Coaching
for Balance

How to
Meet the
Challenges
of Literacy
Coaching

JAN MILLER BURKINS

INTERNATIONAL
Reading Association
800 BARKSDALE ROAD, PO BOX 8139
NEWARK, DE 19714-8139, USA
www.reading.org

The International Reading Association attempts, through its publications, to provide a forum for a wide spectrum of opinions on reading. This policy permits divergent viewpoints without implying the endorsement of the Association.

Executive Editor, Books   Corinne M. Mooney
Developmental Editor   Charlene M. Nichols
Developmental Editor   Tori Mello Bachman
Developmental Editor   Stacey Lynn Sharp
Editorial Production Manager   Shannon T. Fortner
Production Manager   Iona Muscella
Supervisor, Electronic Publishing   Anette Schuetz

Project Editors   Charlene M. Nichols and Cynthia L. Held

Art   Cover Design, Linda Steere; Cover and Interior Photography, © Nathaniel Burkins

The publisher would appreciate notification where errors occur so that they may be corrected in subsequent printings and/or editions.

Library of Congress Cataloging-in-Publication Data
Burkins, Jan Miller, 1968-
  Coaching for balance : how to meet the challenges of literacy coaching / Jan Miller Burkins.
    p. cm.
  Includes bibliographical references and index.
  ISBN 978-0-87207-617-4
  1. Language arts teachers--Training of--United States. 2. Literacy--Study and teaching--United States. I. Title.
  LB1576.B8894 2007
  372.6--dc22
                                                                    2007008219

For the teachers at Chase Street

CONTENTS

1 SECTION
The Job: The Many Hats of a Literacy Coach

2 SECTION
The People: Building Relationships

ABOUT THE AUTHOR

Jan Miller Burkins is in her fourth year as a full-time literacy coach at Chase Street Elementary School, Athens, Georgia, USA. She has worked as a language arts consultant for a Regional Educational Service Agency, a district-level literacy coordinator, a reading specialist, and an elementary classroom teacher. Her work as a consultant has taken her into elementary, middle, and high schools where she has helped school leaders examine their reading instruction, demonstrated lessons, and facilitated professional learning.

In 1989, Jan received her undergraduate degree in early childhood education from Birmingham-Southern College in Birmingham, Alabama, and in 1993, her master's degree from the University of Alabama. She later earned her reading specialist certification and doctorate from the University of Kansas in 1999. Her dissertation, which was a meta-analysis of the research on phonemic awareness, was the Dissertation of the Year for the University of Kansas School of Education and one of three finalists for the International Reading Association's Outstanding Dissertation of the Year award.

Jan is on the Leadership Team of the Red Clay Writing Project, the Athens affiliate of the National Writing Project. She is a member of the International Reading Association, the National Staff Development Council, the Association for Supervision and Curriculum Development, and the National Council of Teachers of English. Jan is currently developing and teaching a literacy coaching course for the University of Georgia. She is a member of two writing communities and enjoys writing poetry and narrative as well as professional pieces. She is also a professional photographer.

Jan lives with her husband, Nathaniel, and her three sons: 11-year-old twins, Christopher and Duncan, and her 4-year-old, Natie. *Coaching for Balance* is her first book.

Author Information for Correspondence and Workshops
You may contact Jan at janelizburk@aol.com.

I n the past five years, literacy coaching has become one of the most powerful strategies for increasing student learning and achievement. Literacy coaches are what I call key "second change agents" (with principals being the first change agents). Although there is considerable literature on the general topic of coaching, there is very little up-close work on what literacy coaches actually do and how they can become more effective. There is even less available written by literacy coaches themselves. It is for this reason that Jan Miller Burkins's *Coaching for Balance: How to Meet the Challenges of Literacy Coaching* is such a gem.

Coaching for Balance is an insider's look at the world of literacy coaching, but it encompasses an outside perspective. It does indeed address balance in every which way. It has heart and mind. The book offers advice for being true to oneself as well as being true to the larger cause, it shows how to be helpful as well as how to foster independence in others, and it promotes individuality of style along with addressing common core essentials.

This is a book that consoles as it stretches. It has great insights that soothe the weary coach as it extends his or her effectiveness. Each of the four main sections is equally powerful. Section 1 deals with the reality of the job by highlighting the tremendous demands and excitement and advising the coach to "take care of yourself" and be true to your own judgment. Section 2 delves into coaching personalities, again furnishing fresh insights on how to integrate the work of the individual coach and the goals of the organization. Section 3 focuses on fostering trust and independence of others, not so much by providing support but mostly by helping teachers develop greater capacity.

Section 4 discusses the import and impact of coaching—why it is so critical for success for all and what it can achieve. The book leaves us with a strong feeling of the emotional force of what it means to be a coach, while at the same time clearly showing that we must use our minds to be fully effective. These days many of us are working on Breakthrough ideas (Fullan, Hill, & Crévola, 2006), namely powerful ideas that will give us breakthrough results in which virtually all students become literate. *Coaching for Balance* makes a substantial contribution to this cause precisely because it is both balanced and comprehensive, showing us simultaneously the inner details and the wider perspective of improving classrooms on a large scale. Read it and reap.

Michael Fullan
Ontario Institute for Studies in Education, University of Toronto
Toronto, Ontario, Canada

Reference

Fullan, M., Hill, P., & Crévola, C. (2006). *Breakthrough*. Thousand Oaks, CA: Corwin.

x

When I first contemplated writing this book, I was intimidated. After all, who is really qualified to write a book? I certainly didn't feel that I was. But as I talked to friends, family, and colleagues, I arrived at the conclusion that I had learned through my experiences at least some information that might help other coaches.

I also noticed that, while the collection of texts on literacy coaching was burgeoning, I had yet to come across one written by a practicing literacy coach. At the time, a couple of coaching books had been written by someone who was once a literacy coach. Others had been written by consultants who did some coaching, program developers who worked with coaches, or by university professors. However, I didn't find a book written by anyone who was broadly dealing with the constancy of coaching.

When I was a classroom teacher, I appreciated most those books written by other teachers. There is something about books written by those still "in the field" that brings with them a certain sense of hopefulness. The shared experience lends power and authenticity to their texts. I knew that they were like me when they wrote their books. The authors were frustrated, overwhelmed, motivated, curious, and committed, and they knew and thoroughly understood the demands and rewards of my work.

This is not to say that books written by people who work with coaches rather than filling full-time positions in schools as coaches are not valuable. We benefit tremendously from multiple perspectives and, in the pages that follow, I repeatedly refer to these works. It does mean, however, that I really know how you feel. I have experienced the same sense of fulfillment and triumph that grips you when the many scattered pieces of an endeavor find their home within the puzzle of school change. I have also wanted to throw my hands up and quit, have struggled with relationship challenges, have let people down and felt the ache of remorse, and have been disappointed by slow progress. I think that currently living in these realities gives me an empathy that is not achieved voyeuristically. This is the same empathy that you, who taught 25 kindergartners last year, have for the teachers in your building. It makes you their advocate, and it makes me yours.

Another trend among authors contributing to the developing coaching literature at the time I began this book was to give heavy attention to reading pedagogy. When I read books about literacy coaching, I find presentations of reading content distracting. I have shelves of books that address how to teach reading. However, my abundant resources dwindle as I search for information about the pedagogy of literacy coaching. My hope is that *Coaching for Balance: How to Meet the Challenges of Literacy Coaching* will contribute to efforts to fill for coaches this pedagogical gap.

Who I Am

I can make a pretty strong case, as apparently I did in my interview for a coaching position, that the varied roles I have served in education have made me uniquely qualified to be a literacy coach. So, while in this book I focus on my last few years as a literacy coach, I am working from a bank of experiences over the past 17 years.

I began my teaching career in 1989, when I was a kindergarten teacher in a self-contained classroom in a small school in rural Alabama. Over the next couple of years, I earned my master's degree in early childhood education from the University of Alabama. In 1995, I began full-time work as a graduate student at the University of Kansas. During this time I served as a graduate teaching assistant and taught the undergraduate "Introduction to Reading" courses.

I finished my postgraduate course work in 1996 and moved to south Georgia where I took a position as a district-level reading specialist. I was responsible for the reading instruction in the school district, and I spent my time facilitating professional learning, visiting classrooms, demonstrating lessons, and conferencing with teachers. I learned a great deal about coaching during this time, both from my mistakes and my successes.

After developing a working relationship with a consultant from our local Regional Educational Service Agency (RESA), I began doing independent consulting work for them and eventually went to work for them exclusively. In this position, I completed my doctoral work in Curriculum and Instruction with an emphasis in reading in 1999, focusing on phonemic awareness with my dissertation work.

As a RESA consultant, I worked in K–12 classrooms in 15 school districts in south Georgia. Again, my position involved work that shaped my literacy coaching experience. At RESA I planned and facilitated professional learning in all areas of language arts instruction and assessment from kindergarten through 12th grade. This also involved working with district and school-level administrators, demonstrating lessons, observing instruction, providing written and verbal feedback to teachers, and conferencing with teachers.

I returned to the classroom in 2001 and worked as an Early Intervention Program teacher for most of a year and a second-grade classroom teacher for a year. In this position, I had the opportunity to receive support from a wonderful literacy coach. This experience of "being on the other side" has been invaluable to me as a literacy coach, as has returning to the classroom full time after years of teaching and learning with teachers. This return to the classroom was an immediate reminder to me that being a classroom teacher is the most demanding job in education. This experience has shaped my coaching experience and dramatically influenced my coaching philosophy.

Finally, in 2003, I accepted the literacy coach position at Chase Street Elementary School in Athens, Georgia, USA.

Common Sense Disclaimer: The Limitations of This Book

Because I am a practicing literacy coach, I know how busy coaches are. So, in a spirit of candor, let me share the limitations of this book. This book will not provide you with an exhaustive choreography for instructional change. It will not tell you how to make a significant impact on reading scores in a short amount of time. It does not present a lockstep, systematic, one-size-fits-all roadmap for literacy coaching in a school community or a comprehensive review of the literature on literacy coaching. Literacy coaches interested in reading pedagogy or in studying the details of a balanced literacy program, as I mentioned earlier, have better options. If you are looking for an easy answer or a sure-fire cure, unfortunately, I don't have it.

On the other hand, if you are reading this book to see a few of the steps others have executed in their dances of change, stay with me through the pages to come. If you are trying to find out how to support teachers in the long-term growth of their understandings of literacy instruction, you may find this book helpful. Maybe you are looking for some honest descriptions of things that have and have not worked in at least one school, or perhaps you want some insight into developing trusting relationships with teachers; if so, keep reading. Even if you are simply looking for some interesting coaching stories or some practical coaching ideas, you are in the right place. Finally, if you are searching for reassurance that you aren't the only one who feels lost and overwhelmed in this work, or if you are simply looking for a little hope, I have some thoughts to share with you.

In literacy coaching, as in most aspects of life, it is risky to make sweeping generalizations. No one owns the truth. Basically, in the context of literacy coaching, the success of any approach or strategy rests largely in the nature and quality of the relationships between the teachers and the coach. What works for one literacy coach as an effective means of supporting teachers may, for another coach, create divisions rather than opportunities for growth. So, while I may speak with authority, for the most part I represent a collective of one. If I say one thing and your instincts tell you otherwise, explore it knowing that coaching strategies are often specific to each school. Consequently, throughout this book, there is one critical underlying premise: Coaching contexts are different and coaches and teachers in any community will map their own paths through change.

I tried to be honest in these pages, both in the things that have gone well and the things with which we have struggled. Seeing that someone else makes mistakes sometimes frees us to take risks. If at times I am painting a perfectly rosy picture, it is just to give you a vision for the ideal. I live in the real world, and while our school community is largely professional and committed, literacy coaches deal with the same personality conflicts, instructional challenges, and sheer exhaustion that other educators face. Just assume as you are reading, and it will be true, that we are also very tired, behind in paperwork, and working at ridiculously high stress levels.

Despite the challenges we still face, our work has turned into a passionate adventure where each day brings with it opportunities for learning and connecting with people. We are in a challenging but rewarding war against poverty, illiteracy, and racial divisions and, after laying much tedious groundwork, I am increasingly excited about the community we are building, the instruction we are delivering, and the children we are teaching.

The philosophy that shapes this book and guides my work as a coach represents my higher self. These are the habits of thought, response, and care to which I aspire. I have written them for you because I believe in them and I trust them, not because I exemplify them. They are a mirror for me to look into to see which professional muscles I am developing and which I need to exercise. Sometimes I meet these ideals. I think that sometimes I even exceed some of them. But more often than not, I wear them awkwardly, like my son stumbling through the house in my shoes. Perhaps, I will eventually grow into them. I speak to you about these habits of practice honestly here, like we are old friends who taught next door to each other for years and you have come to my house after taking a position as a literacy coach and said, "So, tell me what you and the teachers in your school have done that might help me."

It's Hard to Organize a River: The Organization of This Book

The story that follows presents ideas, philosophies, and anecdotes collected from literacy coaching. There are challenges associated with parsing interwoven ideas into separate pieces; it is like trying to cut water with a knife. Writing and life just aren't that neat. While I have sorted themes into separate chapters, there is often overlap as ideas twist and turn back on themselves. Nevertheless, *Coaching for Balance* is divided into 10 chapters that run through four sections. In Section 1, chapter 1 explores the demands of literacy coaching that push and pull a coach in competing directions. Chapter 1 also examines what it means for coaches to align themselves to a philosophy of coaching. Chapter 2 investigates ways to adapt your job to meet your personal and professional needs and offers suggestions for developing a working relationship with your administrator. Chapter 3 encourages you to take care of yourself physically and emotionally. It speaks honestly about the challenges of literacy coaching and supports the premise outlined in chapter 1 that balance is the key to finding joy in and beyond your work.

In Section 2, chapter 4 presents suggestions for developing and maintaining strong relationships with teachers. It also argues the premise that literacy coaches should assume good will of teachers. Chapter 5 discusses the challenges inherent to change. It describes characteristics of change and the role of dissent, and suggests that literacy coaches need to respect the different ways teachers approach change.

In Section 3, chapter 6 addresses the various stages of learning through which teachers often progress as they work to extend their skills and understandings. It also offers ideas to consider when working with a teacher to set priorities for professional learning. Chapter 7 considers the vocabulary we enlist when communicating with teachers, particularly around classroom visits. It offers examples and nonexamples of effective communications and also suggests strategies for keeping anecdotal records of classroom visits. Chapter 8 examines the role of data in the work of literacy coaches. It discusses both collecting and analyzing data and the ways that data can support professional learning and prompt commitment to change.

In Section 4, chapter 9 tells my story of racial identity development and investigates the role of the literacy coach in understanding racial identity and its implications when working with diverse populations of teachers and students. Chapter 10 argues that we should make room for our emotional lives at school. This chapter explores the role of love, faith, and hope in literacy coaching. Finally, the appendix offers reproducible forms that I created and found helpful in my work as a coach.

Perhaps you can make our learning experience your own or use our story of literacy reform to capture your own trends for change. At the very least, I hope you will find a little compassion for yourself when you see how challenging this work has been for us.

With the exception of Section 4, each chapter can stand alone, so you can read just the chapters or sections that relate to your work or you can read them in whatever order most supports your growth. Section 4 deals with particularly challenging issues and needs to be read within the context of the entire book. You need to understand the voice and philosophy of the whole book before you read the final section.

I marked the sections in *Coaching for Balance* with photographs abstractly related to literacy coaching in general and the content of the section specifically. I placed the photographs throughout the book as stones for readers to rest on as they wade across this stream of words and ideas. Each chapter also provides quotes at the beginning and "souvenirs" offered in summary at the end. These, along with the photographs, serve as margins of time and space in which you can rest and reflect.

Considering You, The Reader

The entire time I wrote *Coaching for Balance*, I struggled over when to use *she* and when to use *he*. It made all my work clumsy and impaired my writing fluency. I always empathized with the gender I was leaving out, and I couldn't finish a page without being indicted by my pronoun usage. In an effort to find closure on this issue, I wrote the following poem:

Gender Matters

I give much more thought than I should
as to which personal pronoun is good.

When in writing one cannot use *we*,
one must choose between *he* and/or *she*,

or in some interesting way combine
the two sexes with one slanted line.

I could count them out evenly,
address masses or minorities.

If I use both and then alternate
my writing flow quickly stagnates.

But I think that the point, perhaps,
is not our gender sensitivity gaps

but our clumsy attempts and thought patterns
that teach us about gender matters.

So I will continue to grapple
with Adam and Eve and this apple,

(I thought to say Eve and then Adam
but it upset the poem's nice rhythm.)

but still when I write a new sentence
I will want to give deep pronoun penance

to generations of readers forgotten
when our gender sensitivity was rotten.

I'm just glad there are only two genders.
I hope, now, that I won't omit her (or him).

Despite this metric explanation and my measureless limitations, my effort has been toward equitably considering you. Know that I would like to sit down with each of you individually and tell you this story, but I am hindered by logistical limitations and serious time constraints. Just assume, and it is true, that whatever your race, gender, sexual orientation, religious affiliation, marital status, political bias, shoe size, blood type, hair color, height, weight, age, country of origin, or any combination thereof, I wrote this book with you in mind.

ACKNOWLEDGMENTS

When I wrote the acknowledgments for my dissertation, I was struck by a sense of inadequacy. Once again, as I close the door on another long-term project, I am disappointed in my words. They do not convey the depth of my gratitude nor do they effectively communicate my sense of shared ownership of this book.

My earnest thanks is the only currency I have to offer the many intelligent and kind people who care enough about literacy, coaching, and me to share the best of themselves toward the effort of building this book. It has taken a team to write *Coaching for Balance*, and my team has evolved to encompass a generous collective of quick-witted and kindhearted people. Their contributions have made this work more interesting, more accurate, and more sound; and the fodder of my conversations with them has shaped my thinking across these pages. So to you who have held me up during this process, I speak now with sincerity that I hope reaches beyond the cliché: I truly could not have done this without you. Your fingerprints are on every page.

Peggy, you were the one who said, "You should keep a journal about what you are doing here," and the seed you planted took root. You have truly mentored me over these four years and this book would not exist without the steady encouragement you offer.

JoBeth, you were the first I told of this book and the first with whom I felt safe enough to let read it. You have been my counselor and trusted friend throughout this process and I hope that we enjoy many collaborations in the future.

Coaching for Balance grew from a garden nurtured by a group of poets. To David, Misha, and Dorinne, you were the first to make me feel like a writer. Thank you for your high expectations and your high support.

To my professional writing group, thank you for your valuable advice, particularly for your sensitivity and insight in shaping chapter 9. You guys pushed me when I needed to be pushed.

To my cohort of literacy coaching professionals, I send my unbounded thanks to you. You make me think beyond my thinking, and you are ever patient with my slow processing and my continual, "But what ifs."

I want to specifically thank Scott and Daphne. Scott, you amaze me with your intelligence, your stamina, and your generosity. I hope that I am as smart as you when I grow up.

Daphne, early in our friendship you made a gesture of protection, and I think of you as a refuge still. Not only do you frequently save me from myself, but you also make me feel safe and cared for when the world at large seems threatening. Your presence is always comforting for me, and being in your company makes me happy.

To Nancy, Lindsay, Pat, and Allison, you were the first to voluntarily read this book in its entirety. Thank you for your interest and your feedback, both of which fueled my efforts and made the book better for the readers after you.

To Sarah, you were able to take care of much of the tedium of this book better and faster than I. I deeply value your expertise, honesty, and kindness, and I shudder to think of the shape of this manuscript before you lent your editing and researching skill to its cause. I appreciate the way you became so invested in this project, making it your own in many ways.

Last and most, I thank you, Nathaniel, my library love. Thank you for celebrating this book before I even knew it was growing in my head. When I was overwhelmed with ideas that never seemed to reach their destinations, it was you who I asked in a moment of discouragement, "Do you think I'll ever finish a book?" You replied (Do you remember this conversation, Dear?), "You'll finish many books." You have been and continue to be my truest celebration. From conception to reality, from cover to cover, from beginning to end, you have enabled me and loved me through this effort. Thank you.

The Heart of Coaching

I chose the image of the bike on the cover of this book partially because riding a bicycle requires balance, and partially because teaching someone to ride a bicycle is the classic analogy for scaffolding a learner. Much of the work of literacy coaching mirrors these first efforts at cycling, which many of us have now experienced both as a rider and as a teacher. When I taught my son to ride a bicycle I was initially carrying him, eventually I was just holding onto the back of the bicycle with one hand, then finally I was able to let go and watch. I did not realize at the time that I was moving through a choreography that is descriptive of learning and teaching in many contexts.

Coaches are presently popular in many genres of professional life. Beyond athletic coaches, there are coaches or coach-equivalents in the corporate world, the financial world, the religious world, the construction world, the mental health world, and the physical fitness world. A few years ago, a friend from graduate school called to tell me she was taking a course in how to be a personal coach, and that upon receiving her certification she would be able to coach anyone in anything by supporting them through some universal coaching strategies. As part of a class assignment, she needed to coach someone (anyone) on something (anything). She called to see if I was working on any personal goals toward which she could serve as my coach. I was working on my dissertation at the time and support in completing it was an obvious need.

That was the first time I remember hearing the word *coach* refer to anything other than athletics. I thought it was a lovely idea then, just as I do now. I have many areas in which I want to stretch myself. I would value working with a coach in developing nutritionally sound eating habits, learning to play the piano, and accomplishing my writing goals. What if I had a coach to support me in planning and preparing meals, managing finances, or even relaxing? How would it change my life? Perhaps it would go something like this:

Stepping Up to the Plate: A Play in One Act

Characters
Dishwashing Coach
Messy Adult (yours truly)

The curtain rises in the home of Messy Adult where she and Dishwashing Coach are sitting at a table engaging in a postobservation conference about Messy Adult's dishwashing observation two days prior.

2

Dishwashing Coach: [clearing his throat] Well, the last time I was here, you wanted to talk about areas of the house you felt were approaching crisis level. After our conversation, you decided to focus, for now, on the kitchen in general, and the dishes specifically. You said [reading notes], "If I could just keep up with the dishes and eliminate the rancid smell coming from the sink, I can live with pretty much anything else."

Messy Adult: [insecurely] Yes. That pretty much sums it up.

Dishwashing Coach: [trying to turn conversation over to Messy Adult] Then I asked you if I could come and watch you wash your dishes, to see if I had any ideas about how you could conserve more time and energy in the kitchen. You said, "I would like to spend less time washing dishes and also have a cleaner kitchen." Is that the way you remember our conversation? Is there anything you would like to add about your frustration with the dishes? What have I left out?

Messy Adult: [hesitantly] No. That's it exactly.

Dishwashing Coach [enthusiastically] So...I was here on Tuesday and I watched you wash your dishes. Why don't we

	begin the conversation with you telling me what you think worked well for you?
Messy Adult:	[carrying the weight of her accumulated failures in washing dishes] Not much. I don't really think anything went well. I don't think I loaded the dishwasher right, so I had to wash a lot of the dishes by hand. I didn't prewash well enough, so I had to rewash some of the dishes. Worst of all, the dishes are piled up in the kitchen again, and I'm sure you noticed the odor when you came in, and....
Dishwashing Coach:	[realizing Messy Adult is not ready to articulate her successes at this point] Perhaps, I should tell you the evidence I see that you have made progress toward your goal.
Messy Adult:	[awkwardly] OK.
Dishwashing Coach:	[redirecting the conversation] Well, you wanted to be efficient and conserve time when you are washing the dishes. Let's see, you had 72 dishes to wash and it took you 49 minutes and 12 seconds. That is an average of 46 seconds per dish, factoring in the time for rewashing and cleaning up the broken glass.
Messy Adult:	[afraid of disappointment] Really?
Dishwashing Coach:	[confidently] Absolutely. I also observed several efficient behaviors that you seemed to do automatically. I suspect they contribute to your speed.
Messy Adult:	[beginning to trust] Really? Are you sure?
Dishwashing Coach:	[referring to his written notes] Yes. First, you selected some tools that matched your task. The scrub brush you purchased really fits your hand and is also tough enough to deal with dried-on food.
Messy Adult:	[in a self-deprecating tone] Oh, really? I bought it because I like green.

Dishwashing Coach:	[gently dismantling Messy Adult's efforts to sabotage herself] Whatever the reason, I think it was a sound choice. Also, you took the time to really develop the suds in the sink. By using the hand sprayer you seemed to get more suds.
Messy Adult:	[a little confident] Really? You know, I did notice one thing that worked. I put a little soap and water in the pots and pans before I started anything else. Then I let them soak while I washed all the other dishes.
Dishwashing Coach:	I noticed that by the time you got to the pots and pans they appeared relatively easy to get clean. Were they?
Messy Adult:	[confidence building] Yes, actually. I read about that in the article you gave me. [hesitantly] So do you think I washed the dishes right?
Dishwashing Coach:	[encouraging self-reflection] I'm not sure there is a "right" way to wash the dishes. I think you have to look at the outcomes to determine if your action was "right" in your context. Did the dishes get clean in a relatively short amount of time?
Messy Adult:	[suspiciously] Yes.
Dishwashing Coach:	[pushing for reflection] Was there anything you noticed that you will do differently if you ever wash dishes again?
Messy Adult:	[startled that Dishwashing Coach isn't telling her what to do] Well, before today, I almost never washed the dishes, which was part of the problem. I feel like I'm more likely to wash dishes now. I also think I should rearrange my cabinets, to get the items we use most often closer to the dishwasher.
Dishwashing Coach:	Sounds like you have a plan.
Messy Adult:	[beginning to feel safe] Well, do you have any suggestions for me?
Dishwashing Coach:	[not pushy] You might consider using paper plates sometimes.

Messy Adult:	[empowered] Interesting idea! [pauses to think] Maybe the problem is not that I'm slow in washing the dishes, maybe it's that I have too many dishes to wash.
Dishwashing Coach:	[encouraging continued reflection] You have really reflected on your work and it is seems to have led you to make some potentially productive decisions.
Messy Adult:	[wondering what "reflected" means] Yes. It seems that I didn't really need much help after all. I hope this hasn't been a waste of time for you.
Dishwashing Coach:	[pleased] No, I enjoyed working with you. Perhaps, I can help you rearrange your cabinets.
Messy Adult:	[envisioning the future] That would be great. [pauses] Hey...I think I'll work in the bathroom next. It never seems thoroughly cleaned.
Dishwashing Coach:	Yes. I know what you mean. I just read an interesting article on toilets. I'll copy it for you and put it in your mailbox.
Messy Adult:	[smiling] Thank you.
Dishwashing Coach:	[rolling up his sleeves] So...what do you do in your spare time?
Messy Adult:	[feeling cared for] Laundry!

The curtain falls and stage lights dim as Dishwashing Coach and Messy Adult laugh in the kitchen.

While this play is at once playful and idealistic, it illustrates the potential impact of a coach and captures prominent elements of any coach's job. The content or the technical aspects of a coaching position may vary significantly, but the role of the coach is the same in every domain. It is the coach's job to bring out the best in the student, the athlete, the singer, the teacher, or the dishwasher. If you were my coach, you would need to develop a relationship with me, develop expertise so that you would know how to help me, plan for my success, communicate your confidence in me and my potential, help me find the very best in myself, and, in the end, step out of the way so that I could claim the change as mine.

Efforts on the part of the coach or the coachee are powered by mental muscle, physical muscle, and the biggest muscle of all: the heart. In my opinion, the elements of coaching that render it powerful are those which wander into the emotional spaces of the coachee and the coach. Any goal toward which I sincerely solicit support from a coach represents a corner of my life about which I care. If you help me succeed in matters I manage from my heart as well as my intellect, you have affected my life in potent ways. Tap into my passions and you open doors to my learning that are connected to long corridors of growth and reflection. Open doors of learning for me and you will be moved, too.

Your key to helping me realize the goals of my head and my heart, however, rests in the delicate work of negotiating balance between my need for change and my sense of safety, the encouraging feedback you offer me and the suggestive comments you present, giving me too much of your time and letting change run its course, building my confidence without encouraging dependency, presenting me with facts and presenting me with your opinions, and giving me your all and still preserving yourself.

This list of complex and opposing coaching concerns is just an initiation to what is the most comprehensive and constant challenge of all coaching: Coaching for balance. So, while this book isn't all about balance, balance is all about this book, and its subtle influence is its logical heart. In the chapters that follow, I hope to give you a place to begin searching for your own sense of balance and to reflectively recognize the rhythm that supports your literacy coaching work.

The Job:
The Many Hats
of a Literacy Coach

CHAPTER 1

Checks and Balances: The Competing Demands of Literacy Coaching

"Maintaining your balance is a fluid process."
Julie Morgenstern, *Making Work* Work: *New Strategies for Surviving and Thriving at the Office*, 2004, p. 43

L ittle time on a seesaw is spent with both seesawers lifted eye to eye. Many of us, however, have experienced that lovely moment when there is just enough give and just enough take to hold on to that elusive sense of control. We know that an extra wiggle, a small breath exhaled, or an itch scratched will shift us out of the place where we are suspended in space. Maybe we are just slightly up when a friend is a little down or vice versa. But if we work together we can manage to linger in that almost balanced place long enough to appreciate it and secure a memory of how it feels.

The breathy, suspenseful fun of it, however, isn't in reaching equilibrium while our friends on the adjacent equipment rest in the comforting rhythm of the up and down. The fun is in imagining equilibrium, in being almost there, in recovering from temporary setbacks before one of us hits bottom, in solving an up problem with a little bounce or a down problem with a little push. It's about testing that point of equilibrium, experimenting with push and pull, scooting up and back in the seat, or moving out to the edge, all the while remembering the few seconds when we learned how the middle feels, when we first appreciated the centeredness of sitting motionless on a simple machine that prefers to move. We learn the choreography of stillness, buoyed by energy and anticipation. This work, this taxing, invigorating, frightening, important work, associated with trying to find and hold that level place on a seesaw despite resistance from natural forces, represents nicely the work of being a literacy coach.

Balance Matters

Striving for balance is the sensible approach to everything we do, both at school and in our personal lives. For example, I want my house to be clean, but I want my family to feel comfortable enough at home to live there. I want to engage in stimulating work, but I also want a generous amount of recreation. I need balance in my diet, the books I read, my wardrobe, and the music to which I listen. I need to spend individual time with all three of my children but not too much time with any one.

As Allen (2006) states in *Becoming a Literacy Leader: Supporting Learning and Change*, learning to balance the demands of literacy coaching is the greatest challenge of our work. I think most literacy coaches would agree; balance is the core of our work as we find ourselves positioned between dueling demands. Furthermore, balance is something we strive for in more areas of our lives than literacy instruction and, although it has been overused and misunderstood, "balanced" is still the best descriptor of the work we are doing and the writers and readers we are trying to develop.

Following are a few of the areas in our work that require us to consider competing, critical needs. These are the mental neighborhoods where we ask "Which?" when we visit, and our most accurate but most complex response to ourselves is "Both."

Coach as teacher vs. coach as student. We need to be experts on literacy but we don't need to begin to think that we are *the* experts on literacy or that we are the only literacy experts the school can have. We need teachers to know that we consider ourselves students of literacy. How do we encourage teachers to come to us with specific questions about literacy instruction without communicating that we know everything or that their views are invalid?

Theoretical underpinnings vs. practical applications. We need our coaching to maintain an appropriate mix of theory and practical application. We want teachers to have a theoretical foundation for their decision making, but we don't want to neglect their need for support when it comes to breathing some life into these theories. How do we help teachers build a strong base of understanding about how reading works and why particular instructional decisions are sound, while also giving them what they need to exercise this theory in their classrooms?

Teaching to deep understandings vs. teaching to a program. We want to give teachers a broad knowledge of the reading process that supersedes particular programs adopted by our schools or districts, but we also want teachers to be comfortable with those materials the district requires them to use. How do we help teachers wisely use program materials by evaluating them against their developing understandings of reading theory?

Introducing something new vs. maintaining something established. We need to address the implementation of new initiatives, but we don't need to lose our grip on the improvements we have already made. Getting any new program or promoting any change is going to make learning in that area increase because focus has been shifted in that direction. However, fine-tuning one area means turning away from another. How do we help teachers keep shifting their focus to something new without losing sight of current efforts?

Coach as leader vs. teachers as leaders. We need to demonstrate leadership but not to the extent that others don't develop leadership skills as well. If we have many teachers with many different leadership strengths, our school is in a better position to maintain positive growth. However, this won't happen if we don't get out of the way. How do we know when to lead and when to follow and, in between, how to support developing leaders?

Encouraging positive thought vs. inviting dissent. We need to encourage positive interactions within our learning community, but we don't need to squelch those whose voices of dissent could prevent us from making a mistake. We want to listen to teachers' concerns about impending changes because they will think of potential obstacles that we have overlooked, but we don't want to open the door to contagious negativity. How do we communicate to teachers that we want them to disagree with us without perpetuating persistent negative attitudes?

Working with teachers who want your support vs. working with teachers who don't. We need to concentrate our efforts where we can have the greatest effect on instruction, and that is usually among the teachers who are receptive to our involvement in their work. However, coaches are hired to work throughout a school, and we don't contribute to the development of a school community if we are only working in pockets of the building. On the other hand, if we spend our time trying to push through teachers who are not interested in support from a coach, we risk becoming jaded. How do we develop working relationships throughout the school without becoming frustrated by those who have priorities other than working with us?

Attending to signs of teacher distress vs. pushing for growth. We need to nudge teachers out of their comfort zones, but we shouldn't forget what it's like to be a classroom teacher. We don't want to ask too little of teachers anymore than we want to ask too much. When are their concerns and expressions of dissent necessary growing pains, and when are they an indication that a teacher is in distress? How do we help teachers step into the zone of dissonance that is a prerequisite for growth without overly focusing on the outcome at their expense?

Consistency across classrooms vs. individuality among teachers. We need to push toward consistency across classrooms, but we need to give teachers room to be individuals. There are some basic practices that are sound and grounded in a strong data base, and we want teachers to implement those with fidelity to their defined structure. However, if we begin trying to squeeze all of our teachers into one classroom model, they will be unhappy, and this will affect learning in the school. How do we develop the consistency that counts in classrooms and still give teachers room to make important instructional decisions and let their individuality influence their work?

Supporting district initiatives vs. maintaining school individuality. We need to support the district-level plans for growth while we protect our individuality as a school and our integrity as coaches. Often, district- and school-level initiatives work at cross purposes. How do we advocate for our schools, our teachers, and our children without communicating a lack of support for the district?

Coach as coach vs. coach as supervisor. We need to know what is happening in classrooms, but we need to make sure we don't shift from a coaching stance to an administrative one. This shift is easy to make even when we are being careful. One condescending statement to a teacher can limit the benefits of our coaching. How do we "monitor" classroom progress without assuming a position of authority?

Data collection vs. instructional time. We need to support teachers as they try to base their instructional decisions on sound assessments, but we don't need to let assessment become so time-consuming that instruction is compromised. The most informative assessments are those that teachers administer to individual children. However, these are also the most time-consuming measures. How do we gather just enough data to make valid instructional decisions without encroaching on the time teachers need to spend teaching?

Qualitative data vs. quantitative data. We need to look at qualitative and quantitative data both in published research on literacy and in the work we are doing at our school. We need numbers to support what our eyes and our hearts are seeing, and we need our eyes and our hearts to validate the numbers. How do we keep our data in perspective so that we can learn as much as possible?

Celebration vs. realism. We need to celebrate our progress and work to see what we are doing well, but we don't need to lose sight of where we are going. If we don't really pay attention to the positive work we are doing, we run the risk of losing hope. However, if we are only talking about our successes, we run the risk of stagnating. How do we look honestly at our need for growth while giving ourselves the permission and the emotional space to acknowledge our successes?

A sense of urgency vs. a need for renewal. We need to cultivate a sense of urgency and an appreciation of teaching time in our school, but we need to protect teachers from burning themselves out. The sense of urgency in a school is often positively correlated to the expectations the teachers and leaders in a school hold for children. However, if the culture of the school is relentlessly rushed, the stress level can be destructively high. How do we work within the belief that children are capable of learning every minute that we are capable of teaching, without exhausting all our physical, mental, and emotional resources?

Investing emotionally vs. keeping things professional. We need to develop relationships with teachers that require an emotional investment from us both, but we don't need to let things get so personal that they make our jobs more difficult. The line between our personal and professional lives can grow blurry given the energy and emotion that we share with teachers. How do we respect those boundaries, and do we really have to?

Taking care of teachers vs. taking care of ourselves. We need to make working with teachers our priority but not at the expense of attending to our own professional, physical, and emotional needs. If we give but never stop to replenish ourselves, we will eventually find ourselves without the intellectual, physical, or emotional resources to do our jobs. How do we take care of ourselves in this work while we are taking care of everybody else?

Work life vs. home life. Finally, we need to have the energy to accomplish the emotional, mental, and physical tasks necessary to be happy at home and enjoy our work. We don't want work to seep into our time at home, and we don't want commitments at home to intrude on our time at work. On the other hand, there is an appropriate level of awareness about our home lives that we want to maintain when we are at work and vice versa. How do we attend to our personal and professional lives without compromising either?

So coaches find themselves stretched out across a whole row of seesaws and, more often than not, most of them are leaning more one way than the other. Some may even have one side resting squarely on the ground while the other side is aimed at the clouds. Only a few, if any, are centered and those don't stay there for long. We spend our time working to find stability that is, by definition, elusive. It is then we must recognize that the work does not rest in being balanced. The work is in *trying* to be balanced. We do this by putting careful thought into what we believe about literacy coaching and by using this belief system to help us decide which way to shift our weight.

Defining Our Beliefs About Literacy Coaching

Considering the newness of literacy coaching, the aforementioned polarity of its demands, and the isolation in which most of us work, we are wise to attend to our philosophical foundations before we develop plans of action. In undergraduate or graduate school, most of us had to develop our philosophy of teaching. The exercise of getting a philosophy secured on paper provides one with a powerful opportunity for reflection. The 12 tenets that compose my coaching philosophy follow. Although they are presented as universal truths, they are actually just my perspective. Your philosophy of coaching may be very different and still offer stable supports for your work.

1. I believe that coaches should consider teachers as people before they think of them as teachers. Regardless of the professional encounter, the emotions of the teachers are important and should be a primary consideration of the coach. If a coach compromises the emotional well-being of teachers by offering heavy criticism and little encouragement, the teachers will actually be less able to teach effectively.

2. I believe that the most important element of coaching is relationships. Without the trust of teachers, a coach will never get anywhere in promoting change. Building relationships takes time and putting energy into them is a valid part of a coach's job.

3. I believe that coaches should not take on administrative roles. This is sometimes difficult, especially if a coach's administrator does not understand his or her role. Consequently, coaches must act as the guardians of their positions and their relationships with teachers.

4. I believe that it is the coach's job to assume the best of teachers and others with whom they work. A coach cannot go about this work any other way and be happy. There are too many opportunities to be negative in schools and, in order to have any longevity as coaches, we must decide to give people the benefit of the doubt.

5. I believe that coaches should honor confidences. Coaches should not talk about what they see in classrooms to other teachers—good or bad—without the permission of that teacher. It is rare that a coach should need to talk to the administrator about specific classrooms. If a teacher does not feel that she can trust the coach, the coach will be ineffective. The distress associated with gossip as well as the compromised sense of trust are the byproducts of the unprofessional behaviors of an indiscrete coach.

6. I believe that coaches should advocate for teachers with the administration, with the school district, with other teachers, and even with the teachers themselves. A coach's first obligation is to teachers and he must work to protect them from anything that compromises their ability to do their jobs well. This includes, among other things, unclear or unrealistic demands imposed by district or school-level administrations, hurtful competition between teachers, or a teacher's personal drive toward overextension.

7. I believe that coaches should be advocates for themselves so that they can preserve their physical, emotional, and mental resources to serve teachers. The tasks associated with coaching are endless. Coaches could work around the clock, seven days a week and still leave tasks incomplete. In all likelihood, the school districts would allow this, so literacy coaches must be strict guardians of their personal resources.

8. I believe that coaches should have extensive expertise in the content area in which they are coaching. A literacy coach may not be an expert in literacy instruction, but he or she needs to be close or needs to be putting a lot of energy into becoming one. Coaches need a sturdy knowledge base to be forward thinking in their schools and wisely consider the many facets of schoolwide decisions that will have an impact on student literacy learning.

9. I believe that programmatic and instructional choices should be made based on research. In education, we tend to travel in bandwagons—that is, we adopt instructional programs and methods because they are fashionable. Literacy coaches must resist this urge. Such decisions should be made by informed groups who consider the state of literacy in the school and the quality and volume of research supporting a particular tool.

10. I believe that coaches should support teachers in becoming knowledgeable thinkers and leaders in literacy. Coaches should work toward long-term growth in understandings that influence instruction rather than toward program-specific instructional changes. This promotes a spirit of growth, independence in thinking, and teacher empowerment.

11. I believe that coaches and teachers should find joy in their work. If coaches are not enjoying their work most of the time, something is wrong. The same should be true of teachers. If coaches are intentional about enjoying their work and develop habits and rituals to foster this gratification, they will be able to help teachers do the same.

12. I believe that any philosophy must be exercised within a spirit of balance. If we have no balance in our philosophy of coaching, we run the risk of becoming extremists who live for the philosophy rather than for the people it is supposed to support.

There will be parts of our philosophy of coaching that we will cling to throughout our coaching careers. There are other parts that will change. Much of my coaching philosophy has evolved in the wake of mistakes I have made. Learning from past blunders has made my philosophy particularly meaningful for me. Most of these ideas I have learned through mistakes, so I work to remain closely aligned to them now.

Letting Our Philosophy Guide Us

As we learn from our work, what we read, and the teachers we coach, we amend our thinking in some areas. Our coaching philosophy is, in fact, ours, and we can adjust it as our thinking changes. In fact, if our thinking is not changing, we need to be concerned.

Whether a coach's philosophy is in a static or dynamic phase, she needs to at least know what it is, because a coaching philosophy isn't just a collection of theoretical principles. It is a force that drives and guides decision making on the job and the skeleton on which our job description hangs. What we believe about coaching needs to dictate what we do as a coach.

If our philosophy and our actions are not aligned, moral dissonance will chase the joy out of our work environments. This does not mean we won't make mistakes; we are not perfect. However, we will circumvent error when we can and learn from it when we can't. Outlined below are two coaching experiences, followed by an example from a friend, where I have had to reconcile my actions with my philosophy of coaching.

Being attentive to how teachers feel. When I first took a coaching position, I decided that I was going to be attentive to the feelings of teachers. This meant that I would assume that their current practices were valuable, I would consider their emotional needs within the context of work, and I would wait to ask teachers to change anything until I understood what they were already doing.

One important decision, and it is related to those listed previously, was that I wouldn't have discussions with teachers in which something I said brought them to tears. In a previous position where I gave teachers instructional feedback, I worked from the stance that giving feedback is not about the teachers; it is about the students, and teachers must hear the "truth" regardless of how it makes them feel. In reality, it is very much about the teachers. Those few times that my comments brought teachers to tears were enough to make me examine my philosophy very closely when I began this job. I am pleased to say that since then, as a literacy coach, I have never had an observation or conference with a teacher that left her visibly or emotionally distraught because of something I said or did.

Perhaps this means I'm not facilitating as much change in classrooms as there could be if I were more direct or if I thought more about the children and less about the teachers. There is a school of thought that education should be more businesslike, and that we should be honest with people despite any discomfort it causes them or us. However, many businesses with this philosophy are now failing and they are hiring consultants and coaches to come in and advise them on how the emotional lives of their employees affect their work.

This is my philosophy and it is not an indictment of anyone else's philosophy. If there are change opportunities I'm missing because I err on the side of the emotional comfort of teachers, so be it; the change we traffic on the psyches of teachers is rarely deep or long lasting. Furthermore, this is what I have to do to exist in, even enjoy, this job.

Monitoring word choices. Inevitably, when a group of staff developers meets, someone makes the observation that "working with teachers is a lot like working with children." I'm careful with statements like this, although I understand what people mean by them. The caution of course, is against being demeaning or disrespectful of teachers. While few staff developers would say something like this without the highest of intentions, and while most staff developers have probably had this thought at one point or another, the not-so-subtle implications can communicate condescension.

More accurately, working with teachers in a professional learning situation is like working with any learners in a group. There are universal characteristics of learners just like there are universal characteristics of strong instruction, whether that instruction is for children or adults. So, yes, teaching teachers is a lot like teaching children, not because teachers are like children (as this statement could easily be mistaken to mean) but because children, teachers, artists, athletes, and any others in a group-learning situation have some common characteristics and needs.

My point is that in order to adhere to a philosophy that is respectful of teachers, we have to be very careful with our language. I'm not always successful at saying the most appropriate thing, in fact, I often fail. However, I keep noticing and keep working to make my words and actions align with my philosophy of coaching. I will address this in depth in later chapters.

Establishing boundaries. JoBeth Allen, a friend of mine, is a professor in the Language and Literacy Department at the University of Georgia, Athens. She has been successful in developing her working environment and her instructional role into something that supports her philosophy of teaching and learning and, consequently, into something she enjoys.

For example, JoBeth does not believe it is her job to use grades to judge teachers in her graduate classes. Rather, it is her job to help every teacher learn, and to learn in ways they can transfer to their own classrooms. JoBeth believes that her students will do the work because they want to be strong teachers and because the content is compelling, not because they want to earn a letter grade. She gives students feedback and opportunities to revise all assignments. They have much choice within the course assignments, and she encourages them to take risks.

JoBeth has to submit letter grades to the university, but all her students know from the beginning of the class that she not only expects everyone to earn an A, but that it is her job to help them do so. As counterintuitive as it may seem, this does not make the students work less; it usually makes them work harder. JoBeth's students submit excellent work to her without the motivation of grades. In fact, it seems that not having to worry about grades frees students from the distraction grades create and the traditional game of guessing what the professor wants. Most students live up to her high expectations, and she addresses the rare exceptions individually. This focus on learning rather than grades has made her job more enjoyable for her and helped her align her actions with what she believes about learning and teaching.

The point is not that JoBeth doesn't like letter grades, it's that she has made sure that her day-to-day activities don't put her in a position to compromise her closely held philosophies. This means that she does not have the discomfort, subtle or strong, that accompanies compromising the things in which she strongly believes. In this way, JoBeth has made sure that her work provides her the philosophical room she needs to actually enjoy it.

Recognizing the Importance of Flexibility

Whether you agree with the specific choices in the previous examples or not, I hope the value of living within a philosophy of literacy coaching is clear. If you have been given the opportunity to define your own role, or even if you haven't, I encourage you to act slowly and thoughtfully. Can you shape your work to support your coaching philosophy so that it becomes something in which you believe and about which you can be passionate? Then can you live within your job description flexibly enough to make it work for you?

Of course, there are extremes in any situation and even good things taken in excess can become problems. If we develop our philosophies in cement rather than elastic, we will not be able to differentiate them for individual needs and our consciences will bother us. Sometimes staunchly adhering to a philosophy is actually a violation of it, and it is difficult to break out of dogmatic practices once the concrete sets.

We work in the behavioral sciences and there are few absolutes. The mix of personalities and events that fill our days do not come together predictably. A philosophy adapted to the reality of daily experience can lead to effectiveness and joy at work, while the same philosophy applied rigidly will lead to failure and frustration. We are hired to make a difference in literacy instruction, so our decisions need to exist within these parameters, but the walls that mark these boundaries are flexible, giving you room to breathe.

For example, a coach might decide that he believes it is critical for him to attend to his own professional learning and that he will have nothing to share with teachers if he doesn't replenish himself. This might lead him to conclude that he needs to spend half of each day engaged in his own study and professional growth. Maybe another coach's philosophy dictates that she take care of her emotional health at school, and consequently, she chooses only to work with teachers she likes. These decisions may be aligned with the letter of the coaches' philosophical laws, but they will not keep them employed. Furthermore, such myopic choices grossly compromise the spirit of a philosophy of balance.

On the other hand, a coach can decide that half of one day each week is reserved for professional development. A coach can also choose to spend a lot of her time, at least in her first year, in the classrooms where teachers want her help and are pursuing their own professional growth. These choices allow coaches to practice their philosophies without operating in an extreme.

Where to Begin

While we are working to shape our professional philosophies, we may feel pressure to rush past these reflective efforts and move forward with what others may feel is the "real" work of coaching. For example, a coach may be instantly pressured to monitor implementation of a program, or she may be asked to begin planning professional learning. She may not have any choice in this matter. When they can, however, new coaches need to advocate for the time to reflect on the work they are about to initiate and put sincere energy into defining their current beliefs about literacy coaching.

Generally speaking, change takes time, so there is some margin, particularly in the beginning, for you to reflect and plan. You may never have this opportunity again in your work. Go into your office, shut your door, and read and study for a couple of hours, at least, on your first few days of work. In general, "lay low" for a little while. If it is the first week of school, teachers would probably prefer to establish procedures independent of your support anyway. Hide out in your office and study. After a few days, maybe even a week, visit teachers and look for ways, any ways, you can help them. Then go back to your office and read and plan some more.

In the early days of your job, make contact with people who are in a position to support you: other coaches, consultants, friends and family outside school. You will need them when the work feels heavy. These steps are all critical to building a solid foundation for yourself, and if you skip them now, you may find yourself engaged in the expensive task of digging down and making space for the supports in which you should have invested earlier. It is much less costly, in every sense of the word, to prepare than to repair.

The first task of literacy coaches is to study, plan, read, and get to know teachers and their work. From this, especially if they are reading about literacy coaching in particular, they will begin to develop a vision for their roles. The material available on literacy coaching is now beginning to grow and, by the time this book is published, I imagine that coaches will have many resources to generously support their developing philosophy of coaching.

Choosing Our Battles: For What Are We Willing to Fight?

As happens to professionals in any field, we encounter opinions that are in opposition to our philosophy. The politics of reading can be disturbing and there often seems to be research to support both sides of an argument. With some issues, we already know where we stand. On others, our opinions will evolve from our coaching philosophy and our reflections on our work with teachers.

As literacy coaches read, work, develop, and watch teachers do the same, they inevitably become passionate about some aspects of reading instruction. However, they will be more effective if they reserve their strongest convictions for those issues most important to them. Passion can be a powerful ally or a vengeful enemy. We need to exercise our passions judiciously and only after we have spent much time examining them through the lens of a literacy coaching philosophy.

My friend, Peggy Terrell, was in my office one day talking about her work as a language arts consultant in schools. I enjoy talking with Peggy because she makes me question my assumptions and puts me in the frame of mind to make breakthroughs in my thinking. She said, "I rarely tell anyone that something is the absolute truth. I say something like, 'From what I'm seeing in the schools I work in, this is my current understanding.'" There is always room for someone else to be right and for us to be wrong. If we are frequently declaring absolutes in our work, we are setting ourselves up for disappointment and possibly even embarrassment.

For example, I am passionate about teaching children on their instructional level. If the district commitment that allows me to define this as I see appropriate for my school changes, I will fight for it all the way up the chain of command until I am before the board of education. Instructional level teaching (Betts, 1946) is something I will stand up for as an absolute. Even so, it is my absolute. I feel strongly enough about it that I would look for a different job if my ability to teach from instructional-level materials was compromised by curriculum or philosophical changes in my district. However, there are other issues on which I have definite opinions, but I am willing to bend with differing viewpoints and practices within the school.

This doesn't mean that I work without conviction; anyone who has worked with me knows that I have strong opinions about most aspects of literacy instruction. However, there aren't a lot of issues on which I will weigh in heavily with teachers. I will give teachers material to read, expose them to research, and give them opportunities for discussion. I will even apply gentle pressure in some areas, in the hope that teachers will make the decisions research demonstrates are sound. However, my goal is to develop teachers who know how to think intelligently about literacy, not to develop a school full of intellectual clones.

Souvenirs

The classic push-and-pull of literacy coaching stems from the job's amalgamation of several positions in education: teacher, manager, facilitator, expert, student, and researcher. This fusion results in a tension touching many aspects of a literacy coach's role, and efforts to alleviate this stress dominate our coaching work. While concentrating on parallel opposites, we must let the weight of our philosophical underpinnings influence the rhythm for our work. Living our belief system flexibly and intelligently protects us from a dissolving moral purpose, one that unexpectedly hops off the seesaw and sends us crashing to the hard ground of our conscience.

CHAPTER 2

Creating
Your Own
Environment:
The Coach as an Individual

"[A]ccept the idea that your career can be as unique as your thumbprint."
Barbara Quinn, *Snap, Crackle, or Stop: Change Your Career and Shape Your Own Destiny*, 2001, p. 12

I once had to write a paper for a graduate-level educational psychology course on the ways children create their own environments. There is a theory that, in more ways than we realize, children are in charge of their worlds. Scarr (1992) writes, "each child constructs a reality from the opportunities afforded by the rearing environment, and that the constructed reality does have considerable influence on variations among children and differences in their adult outcomes" (p. 2). The degree to which this is true depends on the circumstances of the home. However, anyone with children is likely to agree that children know how to manage adults. Children know exactly how to get what they want from caregivers and they don't hesitate to be vocal in letting them know that they absolutely loathe Brussels sprouts, they crave strawberry ice cream, or that a crib no longer suits their needs and they would prefer to freely roam the house. Consequently, some children are less likely to have

Brussels sprouts, more likely to have ice cream, and more likely to have the opportunity to explore the house with us running along behind them making sure they don't make serious mischief.

Children are egocentric, and that isn't necessarily a bad thing. Literacy coaches need to think about themselves as well, particularly in the earliest days of coaching. As we are beginning to define our roles, we can push past the discomfort associated with a nebulous job description and find solace in creating our own environments. Let's manipulate Scarr's earlier statement to fit coaching: "each *coach* constructs a reality from the opportunities afforded by the *school* environment, and that the constructed reality does have considerable influence on variations among *coaches* and differences in their *coaching* outcomes."

We Are Pioneers

Literacy coaching has the potential to dramatically change the landscape of literacy instruction in schools, and there is mounting research indicating that literacy coaching is effective. For example, Joyce and Showers consistently demonstrated that teachers transferred new strategies to the classroom more effectively with peer coaching than in training alone (1980; Joyce & Showers, 1982; Showers, 1984). In fact, they found that 95% of teachers were able to reach an "executive implementation" level with a coach, while none of them did this by just studying the theory in isolation or in conjunction with demonstrations; and only 5% reached this highest level of skill when practice was added (Joyce & Showers, 2002).

In surveying teachers who participated in math coaching, Slater and Simmons (2001) found that 29% strongly agreed, and 59% agreed that the experience improved their instructional skill. Research from the Bay Area School Reform Collaborative (BASRC), a nonprofit organization that promotes process-oriented reform in California, presents qualitative evidence that coaching promotes a collaborative culture, increased levels and quality of new strategy implementation, a receptiveness to change, a willingness to take risks, increased school leadership capacity, and a focus on equity goals (Symonds, 2003).

Data are still accumulating, but the results are promising. However, there is some evidence that certain preconditions enhance the effectiveness of a coach. Even-Ascencio's (2002) research suggests that there is a minimum threshold for a school's readiness to effectively use a content coach. Critical factors include a recognition of a problem in student achievement levels, a sense of individual responsibility to do something about the problem and a basic level of trust among faculty members and administration. (p. 248)

Nevertheless, there rests in this role the opportunity to influence classrooms in previously undemonstrated ways. Galm and Perry (2004) describe literacy coaches as pioneers:

What makes you a pioneer? You are in unknown territory.... If other people knew how to interact with faculty at the school level to improve teachers' classroom practice, they would have done it and there would be ample evidence of their success. School-based staff developers would not be necessary. But the very fact that your roles exist is silent testimony that your school systems and schools believe your roles are important. You are the fulcrum of your school systems' efforts to seek better results from teachers' classroom practice. (p. 3)

Given the newness of our positions, coaches have the opportunity to decide exactly how our jobs will look or, at the very least, we have the chance to weigh in heavily as the job description evolves. Galm and Perry go on to say,

You may, however, feel that you are alone, figuring out for yourselves what to do and how to do it, learning as you go.... That is often the case with pioneers, working without support, unrecognized, and unappreciated. Do not be discouraged. Grasp the opportunity to *craft* your new role. Understand that you are on the frontier of professional learning, cultivating new hope among teachers who fear they are not up to the challenges of public education's new demands. (p. 3)

New literacy coaches across the United States are finding themselves in coaching positions where no one can tell them what their job is, so they are crafting their roles. Their principals actually look at them and say, "I don't know why the district hired you" or "I don't know what you are supposed to be doing. Why don't you tell me?" In *Becoming a Literacy Leader: Supporting Learning and Change* (2006), Allen, who has worked as a literacy leader for the last six years, writes, "I entered my current position as a literacy specialist without a job description." She goes on to say that this has "afforded her the luxury of creating her identity as a literacy support person" (p. 2).

Coaches in this situation may have the very understandable feeling that they mistakenly received an invitation to a party no one ever meant them to attend. However, if we can push past our feelings of being unwelcome or unnecessary, then we can recognize and act on the tremendous opportunity to create our own work environments. While we are constantly influencing our work environments, we probably won't have the chance to define our job descriptions so comprehensively again, and once we set our efforts along a particular course, it will be difficult to alter that course.

What Is a Literacy Coach?

Although awareness of the role of instructional coaching in education is growing, there is still much confusion surrounding the work of literacy coaches. If I had a dime for every time I had to explain my job to someone, I would be able to buy the teachers in my school the classroom libraries they so desperately need. Now, when I go to the doctor's office and fill out those personal information forms or I apply for a library card, I don't know what to write in the blank beside "Occupation." If I write "teacher," it isn't really accurate and may even cause confusion. I can be accurate and write "literacy coach," but I will probably end up explaining myself further.

Lately, I've been writing "educator" when I have to complete paperwork, but I always have to stop and work through the previously described sequence of thoughts, usually while my children are dismantling the waiting room. Furthermore, "educator" is the least specific definer of our work; perhaps that is why 89% of literacy leaders have included the word *coach* in their job titles (International Reading Association [IRA], 2006). I do think that "literacy coach" is the most accurate description of the job most of us are doing. The two words represent the two areas of expertise we must possess. So, the next time someone says, "You're a literacy what?" we might respond by saying the following: I am a literacy coach. A literacy coach is an educator with specific expertise and extensive experience in literacy instruction who, through individual coaching, team meetings, formal professional learning, demonstration lessons, classroom visitations, study groups, and various other contexts, works with and for teachers to lead, assist, and honor them as they solidify and expand their skills in and understandings of literacy instruction.

While such a response still won't paint a clear picture, we might enjoy some interesting reactions. Maybe we should print this on one side of a business card and share it with those who stare at us confusedly. On the other side, we could print the following: "A literacy coach helps teachers teach children how to read and write."

A Day in the Life of a Coach

Definitions of and job descriptions for literacy coaches abound (Hall, 2004; IRA, 2006; IRA, Professional Standards and Ethics Committee, 2004; Knight, 2005; Symonds, 2003). Coaches exercise myriad roles in just as many different contexts. However, while literacy coaching bears a sprawling job description, it is a role riddled with specifics. Coaches learn the names of specific children, make specific calculations when examining data, and plan professional learning around specific schedules and specific needs. We work to balance thinking large and thinking small. Sometimes I am struck by the diversity of tasks I face in a given day.

We position ourselves in the middle of the stress associated with change while nudging those around us to work toward its resolution. However, we don't just "see action," we also maintain the camp. We stamp books with the school's name, make copies, and stuff three-ring binders. Our days are filled with mundane tasks offset by complicated interactions and decisions.

A cross section of my day might include working on a draft of a letter to parents that explains our efforts to deemphasize reading levels and focus on reading behaviors; watching a shared reading lesson; examining student writing with a teacher to help her decide where to go next instructionally; locating a book in the library, checking it out, and delivering it to a teacher; studying materials in preparation for a demonstration lesson; meeting with an individual teacher who is in distress; and ordering materials for classrooms. I just jump feverishly among each of these responsibilities that is simultaneously demanding my complete focus. Sometimes I feel productive. Other times I aim at and miss an elusive target. I regularly feel as though I am working too much and accomplishing too little. However, when I consider my work, I inevitably arrive at the conclusion that there isn't anything unimportant enough to let go.

One day I made a list of the various tasks that are a part of my job. To illustrate the scope of a coach's work, I present the list later in this section. First, however, I think it is worth mentioning the tasks I generally don't do. I don't organize or facilitate meetings between parents and all the special-service providers who work with a child. I don't substitute teach. I don't collect or check lesson plans, regularly teach groups of children, or demonstrate lessons while a teacher is not observing. I don't serve car duty, morning duty, or lunch duty. (This is not because I think I am busier than any of the teachers in my school, I just need to be available for teachers during this time.) For the most part, I don't decorate bulletin boards or determine class rosters. I do not evaluate teachers.

While some of these items, like evaluating teachers, are absolute "don'ts," most are general statements. I have served car duty and lunch duty. I have covered a classroom for a few hours when we have found ourselves in crisis for a substitute. The goal is for coaches to develop with their administrator parameters for their work and to still contribute to the efforts of labor that hold a school community together. Nothing will alienate a coach from teachers more than saying, "That is not my job."

In IRA's survey of literacy coaches, coaches reported that they spend the most time in student assessment and instructional-planning activities. Many coaches further reported spending between two and four hours a week in demonstrating, observing, and conferring with teachers ("IRA Surveys Coaches," 2006, p. 3). This is considerably less time than I would suggest spending with teachers and in classrooms. However, every school has different needs, and coaching priorities can vary from day to day. Some weeks for me may be heavy on organizing, planning, and reflecting. Other weeks may be almost completely dedicated to classroom visits and the cycle of feedback that supports these visits. Following are the tasks I do, some with some regularity and some only occasionally. They are organized under the eight "hats" coaches often wear.

1. Coordinate professional learning. I write and submit applications for teachers to receive professional learning credit for workshops; work with administrators to develop professional learning schedules; solicit teacher input for professional learning content; preview instructional videos; develop agendas, protocols, presentations, and handouts; purchase, unload, and set up food for professional learning events; make copies; facilitate learning sessions; organize opportunities for teachers to observe in each other's classrooms; organize and participate in study groups; plan for and participate in team meetings; submit plans, summaries, sign-in sheets, and other documentation to school- and district-level administrators; and tally contact hours and complete paperwork on individual participants so they will receive professional learning credit.

2. Work with teachers on instruction. I visit classrooms; watch instruction; prepare for and present demonstration lessons; engage in pre- and postconferences with teachers when I observe their instruction; complete written feedback on classroom visitations; make copies and file written feedback; develop and maintain systems for managing visitation schedules; write lesson plans; collaborate with teachers as they develop units of study; research and recommend professional resources to support specific teacher needs; and assist teachers in developing and implementing classroom procedures and routines by assisting in efforts to gather materials, make copies, rearrange furniture, sharpen pencils, and so forth.

3. Act as the literacy specialist for the whole school. I develop and promote a schoolwide vision for literacy; organize parent literacy nights; develop summer reading programs; train tutors; coordinate schoolwide genre studies; plan and organize schedules for visiting consultants; support teachers in meetings with parents; complete grant applications; facilitate implementation of the district curriculum; represent our school on district-level committees; assist in developing school and classroom schedules; work with the Family Resource Coordinator, teachers in the English as a Second Language program, teachers in the Early Intervention Program, and administrators; assist in developing and coordinating classroom teachers' visits to other schools; organize our coaching opportunities; and facilitate and participate in the Reading Leadership Team and other literacy-related committees.

4. Manage literacy materials. I solicit materials requests from teachers; work with sales representatives; research and review instructional materials; complete purchase orders; unpack, label, and distribute instructional materials; organize the bookroom; participate in ongoing maintenance of the bookroom; maintain classroom inventories of literacy materials; manage a budget; and work with the media specialist.

5. Participate as a member of the school community. I solicit funds for various projects; write thank-you notes; act as hostess to visitors from other schools; participate in interview committees; write reference letters for teachers; take and share photographs of school events; attend evening events, such as PTA, school musicals, math nights, and so forth; present awards at assemblies; listen to teachers' personal and professional concerns; emcee school programs; participate in the school leadership team; write articles for school newsletters; help teachers with graduate school projects; and support art, music, and physical education teachers as they integrate literacy into their programs.

6. Manage literacy data. I administer individual assessments to children; research and review literacy assessments; train teachers in assessment administration; review assessment paperwork for consistency across classrooms; make copies of assessment forms for teachers; advise teachers on preparing children for high-stakes tests; proctor high-stakes tests; analyze test data; organize data for presentation to faculty; develop action plans based on data; present data to the board of education and community partners; and organize celebrations of progress.

7. Act as a constant student of literacy and of life. I attend professional learning for coaches; read professional materials; write in response to professional readings; meet with coaches from other schools and engage in professional dialogue; research and review websites; try to keep up with current periodicals; develop my professional goals; and reflect on my learning and my work.

8. Manage time and resources as an employee of a school district. I write and respond to e-mail; input data; develop documents; organize my professional resources; manage my calendar; participate in my evaluation; complete various school- and district-level forms and paperwork; keep up with a running to-do list; collect and manage paperwork from teachers; file documents; sort through mail; make phone calls; keep a log of how I spend my time and submit it to school- and district-level administrators; and even dust my office.

While extensive, this list is not exhaustive. The critical element is not, however, how long the list is, but how much of a coach's time a task demands. For example, I spend a lot more time demonstrating lessons than I do making copies. The tasks that involve directly working with teachers are the most critical, in my opinion. We need to be judicious in how we spend our time, saving most of our energies for the efforts that will directly affect instruction. The difficulty is, however, that it isn't always obvious which efforts those are.

I hope the list above communicates a sense of the working life of a literacy coach. I'm not certain how alike or different my job is from other coaches, but I have yet to meet a coach who doesn't feel overwhelmed and pulled in many competing directions. At the same time, this is the most gratifying position I have ever held.

Ours Must Be Jobs for Wonder Women and Supermen: Expectations for Literacy Coaches

The school communities' expectations of literacy coaches are still evolving despite the fact that the demands are already deep and wide. Guiney (2001) states,

> This is not work for the faint-hearted. To do it well requires a calm disposition and the trust-building skills of a mediator combined with the steely determination and perseverance of an innovator. Add to this mix the ability to know when to push and when to stand back and regroup in the long-term process of adopting new approaches to galvanize a school to function differently. To succeed, a coach must be a leader who is willing not to be recognized as such and, at the same time, who is able to foster leadership among teachers who rarely regard themselves as leaders. (p. 741)

Given the difficulty intrinsic to the job of literacy coach, there is a serious risk that, as funding for literacy coaches outruns our knowledge of what does and does not work in coaching, and the abilities of colleges and universities to provide specific, intense training in literacy, the integrity of the literacy coach position can be compromised. Bean, Professor of Learning and Instruction in Reading Education, states,

> There is irony in the fact that we have certification for reading specialists to work with struggling readers but do not have the certification for those who should be knowledgeable as a specialist and, in addition, have the

leadership skills necessary to work with teachers, administrators, and parents. (as cited in "IRA Surveys Literacy Coaches," 2006, p. 2)

In its position statement on the role and qualifications of reading coaches, IRA (2004) addresses this concern:

Reading coaching is a powerful intervention with great potential; however, that potential will be unfulfilled if reading coaches do not have sufficient depth of knowledge and range of skills to perform adequately in the coaching role. Education reform is riddled with examples of potentially powerful interventions that disappoint reformers and fail the students they are intended to help. (n.p.)

So what are the qualifications for these educational superheroes? Coaching is the amalgamation of many jobs: teacher, manager, writer, thinker, planner, secretary, researcher, student, coach.... Nevertheless, coaching can be represented by a few universal characteristics. Based on my experience, following are the four traits I believe are most critical for a literacy coach. The relationship among these four traits is illustrated in Figure 1.

1. A coach must have content expertise. I use the word *expertise* because it is broader than the word *knowledge*. A person can accumulate content knowledge from books; but to gain expertise, she must actually put ideas into practice. Literacy coaches must know a lot about literacy and adult learning theories, and they must have experience in teaching children and adults. Theory and experience combined give the coach expertise. Content expertise is an obvious requirement when hiring a coach, however, in and of itself, said expertise won't necessarily make someone a strong coach; "just as great athletes don't always make great team coaches, great teachers don't necessarily make great literacy coaches" (Coskie, Robinson, Buly, & Egawa, 2005, p. 60).

2. A coach must have relationship competence. He must positively support learning and communicate respect. Such a coach provides "companionship and support in dignified inquiry" (Joyce, 2004, p. 82). This is broader than the general statement "works well with people." It includes an understanding of balance, concern for the whole teacher, the ability to assume the best of people, the ability to foster trust in teachers, an

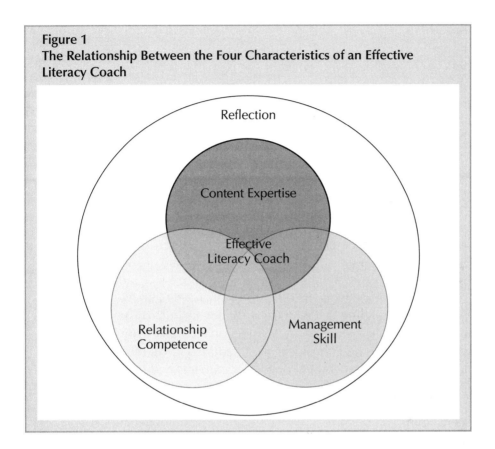

Figure 1
The Relationship Between the Four Characteristics of an Effective Literacy Coach

Reflection

Content Expertise

Effective
Literacy Coach

Relationship
Competence

Management
Skill

awareness of one's limitations, a durable sense of self-worth, a drive for self-preservation, a commitment to excellence, and at least a little self-control.

3. A coach must be an efficient manager. The management requirements for coaches are endless: management of paper, management of time, management of schedules, management of funds, management of electronic documents, management of books, and so forth. Basically, a literacy coach must be organized. There are so many components of our coaching work, each vying for our undivided attention, that balancing them is a challenge for those who are organized and an impossibility for those who are not.

4. A coach must be reflective. Reflection is the most important quality for a coach because it is the glue that shapes the other three characteristics into a permutation that will render her effective. Reflectiveness should be the wallpaper behind every picture a coach hangs within the room that is her coaching philosophy, whether she is giving feedback on an observation or making decisions in purchasing materials.

Reflection is the surrogate of analytical thought. Reflection identifies a problem that a coach must then analyze. If coaches are not reflective, they have only a superficial understanding—if that—of the complexities of their work. In fact, a lack of reflection can be the ruin of a coach and a school. There have been entire reform efforts that have failed largely because they failed to study themselves (Joyce, 2004). Certainly, failure to reflect contributes to failure to move forward. On the other hand, when our "self-corrective capacities" (Schmoker, 2004, p. 88) are realized as automatic patterns of thought that constantly process and reprocess events, look for patterns, push beyond barriers, and create paths to understanding, we enable ourselves toward success.

Reflectiveness affects the other three qualities of an effective coach. We reflect on reading behaviors and literacy instruction and weigh them against our content expertise; we reflect on a conflict with a teacher to identify its causes and consider how to address it; we reflect on the amount of time we spend looking for documents and decide to reorganize our files. Basically, reflection is the constant evaluation of ourselves and of our work. Reflection, however, takes time, and hours spent "thinking" don't read well on a time log. In all likelihood, a coach will have to advocate for the space and time to reflect.

Bringing Your Administrator on Board

No one is as critical to a school's attempts to reform literacy instruction as the principal. I have not talked to a single literacy coach who doesn't find this to be absolutely true. Administrators can facilitate change, interfere with change, or just communicate indifference by failing to invest in change. Either of the latter two is a problem and severely limits the progress of the school, despite the presence of a coach.

In terms of literacy leadership and the work of a coach, we have to shape ourselves to complement our administrators wherever possible. To a large extent, our administrators will decide how our job will look and how we will spend our time; it is critical that we understand their administrative styles. Following I list the four types of administrators I

Table 1 Administrative Styles of Working With Literacy Coaches		
	Active	**Passive**
Informed	Active and informed	Passive but informed
Uninformed	Active but uninformed	Passive and uninformed

have observed and the behaviors that define their administrative styles (see also Table 1).

1. Passive and uninformed. She has only a superficial concern for the literacy instruction in the school, if that. She knows little about literacy or what is going on in classrooms. For the most part, she will leave a coach to do his job without her involvement. If you ask for her support, she might help. It is probably safe for a coach to speak with her, but she generally doesn't hear him. Such an administrator is likely to impede the work of a coach.

2. Active but uninformed. He is very interested in the literacy instruction in the school. However, he does not take the time to learn about literacy, the coach's efforts with teachers, or the instructional practices already in place in the school. He simply acts, and his impulsivity makes him dangerous. He may decide to purchase a literacy program without seeking the literacy coach's input, or he may give teachers suggestions that are not instructionally sound. If the literacy coach asks for support, the administrator might try to help, but he may actually make her job harder in the process. He is too busy to truly listen to a coach's concerns. Such an administrator can be debilitating for a coach.

3. Passive but informed. She truly cares about the school and is a sound administrator. She tries to learn about literacy instruction, and she seeks the literacy coach's input on decisions that affect literacy instruction in his school. She is aware of the strengths and struggles of the teachers in her building. However, this administrator trusts the literacy coach's judgment and pretty much leaves him to do his job without interfering. If the coach suggests that the administrator implement a particular action to improve literacy instruction, she will do so with little persuasion. If you ask for administrator support, she is eager to help. Such an administrator is likely to facilitate a coach's work.

4. Active and informed. He truly cares about the school and is a sound administrator. He is knowledgeably supportive of the coach's efforts and trusts her judgment, but he wants to be fully informed of her work and to understand why she thinks a particular action is warranted. He is eager to act, but talks with the coach before moving ahead on decisions that might affect literacy. This administrator competently supports instruction, making recommendations that reinforce her work. Although working with him may seem cumbersome at times, it is worth the effort to work with an administrator that is knowledgeable. He listens to the coach, and if she needs help, he will think creatively to secure it for her. It is safe to disagree with this administrator. He understands or is willing to learn how to work with a coach as part of an instructional support team. Such an administrator is likely to enhance a coach's effectiveness and promote a coach's professional growth.

Ways to Work With an Administrator

An unsupportive or ineffective school administration can hinder coaching efforts to the point that coaches feel they have failed. In fact, while teaching skill and classroom experience are important for an administrator, more important is "their 'cheerleading' function and their willingness to 'carry the flag' prominently" (Joyce, Murphy, Showers, & Murphy, 1989, p. 74). If our administrators are not backing up what we say, visiting classrooms to observe the work of teachers, and expecting the school's instructional efforts to bring change, we have to understand how this will limit our effectiveness so that we don't grow too discouraged.

This is not to say that it is impossible to make a difference as a coach in schools where the administration is not strong. It just means that this difference will most likely be slower and harder earned. Literacy coaches in this context should build strong supports for themselves because their work is likely to be even more fatiguing than that which is inherent in all literacy coaching. Preserving ourselves must be a high priority. Toward this effort, following are a few suggestions for developing a relationship with your administrator.

Communicate regularly. If you can, set regular meeting times with your administrator. These meetings may be frequent and short or periodic and longer in duration. Depending on the administrative style of your principal, you may need to keep careful notes about what you have discussed with him.

Speak up. Go ahead and say it. Coaches need to tell administrators when they are uncomfortable with their actions or when their requests are interfering with their work. Whether they listen or not, speaking up for what we want or need can be a critical step in getting what we want or need.

Be specific. The bigger the issue is for a coach, the more important specificity becomes. Tell your administrator exactly how he can support your work. Literacy coaching is relatively new to the field of education and administrators are likely to be appreciative if we tell them how they can help us.

Help her become a literacy expert. The more an administrator understands about literacy the more she will understand the coach's work. If she understands the work, she will be less likely to create obstacles for the coach. Building an administrator's theoretical understandings around literacy and coaching may be a slow process, but it will eventually lead to enhanced job efficiency for both the administrator and the coach.

Make his job easier. As your administrator begins to recognize your competence, he may ask for assistance in areas other than literacy. If these requests do not compromise you as a coach, and if they are not excessive, you might try to be helpful. Developing a working relationship with an administrator is much like developing a working relationship with a teacher. The relationship is as important as the work, and one way to develop a relationship with someone is to roll up our sleeves and help.

Help teachers become better at teaching children to read and write. If we positively affect literacy instruction, everyone in the school will benefit. The children will read better, the administrator will be cast in a positive light, the school will get positive attention, teachers will be encouraged, we will get to do our jobs without impediment, and everyone will be motivated to continue pressing forward.

Leadership Without Authority

Leadership is a trait usually attributed to the person in charge, in our case, the principal. However, literacy coaches exist in a gray area, which can prove trying. We shoulder the responsibility of leading the faculty in literacy change, but we don't have the authority to tell anyone to do anything. It is critical that we remain in this uncomfortable grayness rather than wander into the relative clarity of an administrative role or in the other direction where our work lacks specificity and direction.

When an administrator says to a teacher, "Why don't you put up a word wall and see how it supports your writing instruction?" the teacher may hear "The next time I come into this room I want to see a word wall up!" or "Put up a word wall right away!" Administrators, by virtue of their positions, have a subtext to everything they say to teachers. This subtext brings with it an innate urgency.

Any sense of urgency we create has to come from some place other than our authority. It is hoped, however, that we will have earned the right to weigh in heavily on such things as schedule changes or guided reading-group assignments. This right should come from the attention we have drawn toward data, the evidence that we have expertise that makes our opinions worth listening to, and the relationships we have developed with teachers. This authority is hard-earned, and we won't claim it overnight. In the meantime, we must make sure we understand the difference between our role and that of the administration, and listen more than we talk.

Our job is not to make sure that teachers are teaching; it is to support them as they improve their instruction. It is not our job to go through the school to check to see if everyone is teaching a particular program. It is our job to provide professional learning on using said program and to go into classrooms to support teachers as they implement it. It is also our job to make sure that the teachers have the materials they need to teach the program.

Maintaining the distinctiveness between coach and administrator can be a challenge. The line between the two is fine and it is easy to inadvertently step over it. Toll (2004) explains,

[C]oaching is new to the culture of many schools, and staff members often feel suspicious about claims that the coach is there to help. In such situations, when a coach behaves like a supervisor, even subtly, those suspicions flare and the entire coaching endeavor is compromised. (p. 6)

Keeping clear boundaries between the role of the coach and the role of the administrator is difficult. Literacy coaches are relatively new to schools, and we don't fit anywhere on the organizational chart. We are hierarchically homeless and, because this relationship with the rest of the school is ill-defined, we have to constantly question our work and examine our practice. We must watch ourselves and err on the side of caution when we are making decisions about how to relate to teachers. Policing ourselves is difficult, because it is easy to shift focus and begin policing teachers to promote our own agendas, or those of our principal, school district, or both.

Policing for Ourselves

It is possible to fall into the trap of taking on a supervisory role because of pressure we put on ourselves. We may find ourselves tempted to overreach if we have our sights set on some effort. If our focus is on implementing a particular practice rather than on the teachers who are implementing it, we may experience an urge to act like an administrator. My coaching colleague, Scott Ritchie, calls this "coaching the teaching rather than coaching the teacher." We must be extremely careful. We may have some immediate gratification, but the long-term effect of stepping into the shoes of the administrator will surface in compromised relationships with teachers. Just because we can't see the undertow, it doesn't mean that it isn't there or that it can't swallow us whole.

Perhaps a literacy coach favors a certain program—I'll call it The Super Sight Words Program—and passionately believes that if teachers will just use it as the publisher prescribes, the children in her school will all learn the sight words assigned to their grade level and develop the automaticity they need to be fluent and reflective comprehenders of text. Perhaps the district has even adopted The Super Sight Words Program. And maybe a particular teacher is not correctly using the felt finger puppets with the sight words on them. Imagine that the coach has modeled their use several times. Imagine that she believes the teacher just doesn't like The Super Sight Words Program and that, when the coach is not in the classroom, he isn't using it at all.

Then imagine that the literacy coach gets frustrated because she knows the children need to know their sight words. She loses her patience with the teacher and tells him he must do The Super Sight Words Program as prescribed and that she will be visiting his room everyday "to support him."

This is an example of coaching the teaching and not the teacher. In such cases, the literacy coach ignores the teacher's feelings and opinions. She might, instead, explore why the teacher does not like The Super Sight Words Program or how he would prefer to teach sight words. Perhaps the teacher just needs additional sincere support. Maybe the coach needs to demonstrate how to use the finger puppets again. Or maybe this teacher's students have been mastering their sight word lists for years, and the literacy coach just needs to administer some assessments to understand that the classroom teacher already knows how to successfully teach sight words. Regardless, the teacher has the right to make instructional choices within his classroom. If these are in violation of school or district instructional policies, it is not the coach's place to enforce these policies.

Once again, balance is critical in managing the delicate work of supporting teachers while influencing classroom performance. The extremes, again, are the most dangerous ends of the seesaw. The balance between monitoring and coaching is most easily achieved for me when teachers have clearly stated a commitment to adopting a practice. Then I have the freedom to police for the teacher. I can say, "I'm pointing this out because I know you are committed to making this strategy your own."

In our school, the teachers chose to adopt guided reading before I was ever hired. I have a commitment to helping them implement guided reading with fidelity to the structure that defines it and with integrity to themselves. I am pushy in these professional areas, but I am ever mindful of the teachers and what I know about them as individuals.

Policing for Our Principals

While literacy coaches are watching out for their own accidental blurring of the literacy coach–administrator distinction, their administrators may ask them questions or direct them to do something that they feel might strain their relationships with teachers. A principal may say, "I have asked primary-grade teachers to do interactive writing with their children every day in the way you demonstrated in our professional-learning session. What is your sense of how completely they are doing this? Is there anyone who is not doing it?" The literacy coach will, of course, have to respond. This is obviously a delicate situation. The principal is our boss, but we as literacy coaches must work for and with the teachers or we will ultimately fail.

My response would depend on my comfort level with the administrator and the degree to which implementation is in place. If I am working with an administrator who understands the delicacy of my role, I might be completely frank about what I thought was going well and what was still an obstacle for us. On the other hand, I might say something like, "Most grades seem to be implementing interactive writing in some fashion. If you want to get a strong sense of how interactive writing should look in the classroom, I suggest you visit second grade. I have some concerns about a few teachers, but I am scheduled to work with them heavily next week."

I would talk with the administrator about a specific classroom situation only if it is truly serious and if I have exhausted all other resources at my disposal in an effort to effect change. Our principals have the power to help us, such as hiring a substitute so that we can work one-on-one with a teacher or take him to visit another school, purchasing other support materials, or giving a teacher a release from his duties in order to focus on a particular challenge. We must proceed with caution, however; our principals also have the power to quickly dismantle our long-term efforts.

Another response to the aforementioned question would be to say, "I have been working in individual classrooms and have only a general idea of the big picture at this time. My global observation is that most teachers are beginning to implement the practice. Everyone is at least jumping in and trying, and I am supporting them where they need clarification and modeling. If you are interested in a clearer picture, you might visit classrooms and look at the products that are developing from their interactive writing events. In particular, look for...." This lets the administrator know what she should look for in order to get her own answer to the question.

If my relationship with an administrator were young and I was trying to establish boundaries and clarify my role, I might say, "I am uncomfortable working in a supervisory capacity with teachers because then they will feel that I am evaluating them and they will not trust me. I would prefer to continue trying to raise the level of understanding around interactive writing so that you can focus on the level of implementation and teachers will continue to be comfortable with me in their classrooms." You might also let the administrator know that you are willing to give him or her individual professional learning on interactive writing.

"More direct linkages between professional development and accountability will fail—or at the very least will be relatively ineffective—to the extent that they turn professional development into a tool for control" (Elmore, 2002, p. 12). If professional learning, in groups or in classrooms with individual teachers, is about forced and policed work, it will compromise our relationships with teachers and lead only to superficial change.

Another example of policing for the school-level administration involves lesson planning. If a literacy coach works in a school where lesson plans are turned in to administrators, it is not his job to collect, check, or respond to them. It may be the literacy coach's job, however, to make sure teachers understand how to most easily document in their lesson plans the work they are doing in their classrooms. It might even be his job to, upon request, help the administrator understand what he is looking at and for in lesson plans, although there are probably teachers who could do this task with less risk. The literacy coach might decide to develop sample lesson plans, make sure the principal approves of the format and the content, and then share them with the teachers. He will probably be asked by individual teachers to read over their lesson plans to see if he thinks they are sound or if he thinks they meet the principal's expectations. A teacher asking the literacy coach to read her lesson plans is very different from the literacy coach reading that same teacher's lesson plans because the administrator wants him to check them.

Policing for the District

Sometimes the roles that compromise our work with teachers will sneak up on us. One place where the coach–administrator role can get really blurry is around district policy. If the school district has mandated that teachers use a certain program, district-level administrators may ask us, a logical choice, to verify that it is being used. This may seem sensible to the school district, and I can certainly see the practicality of it. However, if this is a common practice, teachers will see us as the enforcing arm of the school district. School-level administrators should be the ones telling the teachers what the district expects of them. We should be making sure the teachers understand *how* to do what the district asks, and that the administrator knows what she should see happening in classrooms.

Telling administrators that our role does not include monitoring can be particularly sticky. The district-level administration, to varying degrees, evaluates the literacy coach and the principal by teachers' levels of program implementation. If teachers are supposed to be using the Bumble Bee Phonics Program and the district asks us to find out if, in fact, they are Bumble Bee-ing, then the teachers are not the only ones in a vulnerable position. However, the acts of monitoring and coaching should bring opposite emotional responses from teachers. Coaches who engage in such paradoxical behavior can significantly impair the progress of their school.

Furthermore, a coach may encounter philosophical differences with the school district. At what point does what the district asks us to do and what we know we need to do become so diametrically opposed that we can no longer do our work? This is worth considering before the situation arises. We will be happier in our work if we can operate within the philosophical framework we have defined for ourselves. A coach needs to know the issues on which he can bend and the issues for which he will fight.

Making Hard Choices

While we may remain silent on issues that weigh on us as coaches, we need to speak out on issues that weigh on us as human beings. I am referring to situations where teachers are cruel or somehow inappropriate in their interactions with children. There may be times when we need to make decisions that put us in tense circumstances. Because coaches are in halls and classrooms a lot, probably even more than administrators, we sometimes see behaviors that make us uncomfortable. This discomfort is rooted in our humanity, and the energies we exert toward addressing it come from a place of compassion rather than a place of authority. These are the incidents that we would feel just as compelled to address if we saw them from the vantage point of a classroom teacher.

The difference is that the classroom teacher is largely isolated and has a limited range of view. She can close her door and not see the offending behavior any more. Coaches on the other hand see much, and they are not able to hide from it. Taking a stand on extreme issues does not mean that the literacy coach is monitoring the general behaviors or work of the teachers. Issues of abuse, cruelty, or severe unprofessionalism are different than issues of general instruction.

Incidents of teachers physically hurting children are largely clear-cut. Teachers berating or yelling at children are often more subtle acts and become more difficult to address. Most educators know that there are times when teachers need to be firm, even animated, with children. However, observing persistent yelling, a teacher getting into a child's face and belittling her, or a teacher grabbing or pushing a child, can present the literacy coach with an ethical dilemma. Furthermore, the odds are good that the coach will see the particular behavior again if she doesn't address it.

Perhaps a literacy coach is in a school that has developed a culture of tolerance when it comes to dealing with children harshly. If the coach is new to a school, he might find himself in an awkward position where behaviors with which others have grown accustomed make him feel sick. However, doing nothing can lead to chronic discomfort, and it is better for a literacy coach to do the hard thing than to become calloused himself.

I once left a job because I was very uncomfortable with the way many teachers were responding to student misbehavior, and I felt powerless to bring about change. I decided then that, regardless of my role in a school, I would not ignore unprofessional, unkind, or downright mean behavior directed toward children. Furthermore, I would not, as much as my situation would allow, work in a place where these attitudes were a recurring theme that the administration consistently ignored.

Once as a classroom teacher, I worked adjacent to someone who was harsh with children. This was not blatant abuse; it was more of a subtle, erosive way of communicating with children that regularly left them in tears. I listened to as much of it as I could before I talked to the teacher and submitted a letter of concern to the administrator. As it turned out, there had been other complaints about this teacher. Needless to say, this action left my relationship with the teacher severely strained. However, this discomfort was less than the discomfort I would have felt if I had chosen not to act. As a coach, I have experienced similar situations.

Coaches need to have an emergency plan in case they do encounter a situation where a teacher demonstrates inappropriate behavior with children or gross negligence on the job, and the literacy coach feels compelled to act. I think this is true for classroom teachers as much as it is for literacy coaches. The difference is that we are exposed to more of everything, for better or for worse.

Souvenirs

Literacy coaches have both the luxury and the challenge of living and working within an evolving, sometimes even unstable, job description. The risks and opportunities that test our content expertise, our emotional integrity, and our managerial skills position us to productively reflect on this virtually indescribable work. Despite a blurry job description and a pervasive sense of feeling overwhelmed, we are on the cusp of dramatically affecting the lives of students, teachers, and ourselves. Much of our success in these efforts rests in our ability to work effectively with other members of our school team.

CHAPTER 3

Taking Care of Yourself: Conserving Your Personal Resources

*"Everyone who has sold himself wants
to buy himself back."*
Mark Strand, "The Way It Is," *Selected Poems by Mark Strand*, 1990, p. 81

I f a mother is traveling by airplane with her child and there is trouble with the cabin pressure, she must give herself oxygen first so she is able to give oxygen to her child. Similarly, in literacy coaching, we are obligated to take care of ourselves so that we have the resources to help others.

While it may seem selfish (but it's not), we cannot take care of teachers if we do not take care of ourselves. If we are fortunate, we will have an administrator who takes care of us. However, we have to commit ourselves to the challenge of overcoming the host of barriers to self-care that are intrinsic to literacy coaching.

Coaching requires relentlessness, but we need to develop some strategies for keeping ourselves balanced. For me, the challenges of coaching are offset by the variety of the work. If I'm exhausted from observing, I can plan professional learning. If I am fatigued from planning, I can study. One minute I am trying to raise funds to purchase classroom libraries, the next I am demonstrating a guided reading lesson, and the next I am testing a child. Variety in my work gives me more stamina.

Nevertheless, coaching can be detrimental to your health. There have been reports of administrators discovering the skeletons of literacy coaches in the bowels of schools, fingers stiff with rigor mortis, still clutching some text in preparation for professional development they may need to facilitate in the afterlife. This is, of course, written with a bit of sarcasm, but there is an underlying vein of truth. Literacy coaching is physically, intellectually, and emotionally demanding work, and it will take its toll on you if you let it.

Who Takes Care of Us?

Most educators would agree that school districts are notorious for letting educators burn themselves out. One study shows that after five years, up to 50% of new teachers have left the field (Ingersoll & Smith, 2003). Meanwhile, the teachers who remain endure disgruntled administrators, accusing parents, and politicians ignorant of the realities of education. In education, the work is never done, and we are salaried employees rather than hourly wage earners—that is, we are expected to work until the job is done and it never is.

If we let it, literacy coaching will seep into every crevice of our lives until we are completely saturated by it. I think there are times when our work can be so rewarding that we can no longer tell what is recreation and what is work. This is lovely, but the reality is that setting work limits for ourselves is wise. As the saying goes, a star that burns twice as bright lasts half as long. We are wise to save a little of our light for the people in our personal lives.

When I was working as a language arts consultant, I had a wonderful boss. He was a gifted manager of people. He realized what should be obvious in the world of work: If he took care of us, we would do a better job and be happier while doing it. If we were happier in our jobs, then strong candidates would compete for positions in his organization. If he was able to get the best people, his organization would be stronger, and he could do his job more effectively.

His care for us made us loyal. We had so much respect for his professionalism and so much appreciation of his thoughtfulness toward us that when he did need us to stay late or put in extra hours, we were eager to do it and grateful for the opportunity to demonstrate our commitment. In this position, I learned how preserving myself—even working less—could actually help me do my job better. This fact has been well-documented in the literature on productivity (Loehr & Schwartz, 2003) and is at the forefront of current business thinking.

Unfortunately, however, the mentality of overworking the people who are taking care of an organization is on the rise. For example, writer, researcher, and social commentator Barbara Ehrenreich went undercover to see if she could actually live in big cities in the United States while working in a low-wage job. She details her experience in her New York Times best seller, *Nickel and Dimed: On (Not) Getting By in America* (2001). Ehrenreich cites Moody, who argues in his book, *Workers in a Lean World: Unions in the International Economy* (1997), that rising stress levels at work "reflect a new system of 'management by stress' in which workers in a variety of industries are being squeezed to extract maximum productivity, to the detriment of their health" (p. 35). Ehrenreich goes on to describe on-the-job situations that negatively affected her physical health (e.g., not being allowed to go to the bathroom) and her emotional health (e.g., unannounced purse searches).

Think about it. How many times have we, as classroom teachers, compromised our health by not eating (or eating too fast), not drinking enough water (because it will make us need to use the restroom), or not going to the restroom (because we can't leave our students)? How many times have you experienced the emotional strain associated with being blamed for the woes of education, even of society? These negatives associated with teaching take their toll on teachers, which then takes its toll on a literacy coach.

The first year in a school is usually the hardest for a literacy coach, and my first year was not any exception. However, when the job is hardest and most invasive is the most vital time to strategically plan for our recovery. The harder the job, the more important it is to set limits and schedule time to renew. In *The Power of Full Engagement: Managing Energy, Not Time, Is the Key to High Performance and Personal Renewal*, Loehr and Schwartz (2003) write, "At the most practical level, our capacity to be fully engaged depends on our ability to periodically disengage" (p. 38). So, disconnect. Unplug the cord that attaches you to the school and acts as a power source. You have access to energy sources that are far more efficient and less expensive.

We Do Not Have to Be Perfect

Most coaches I know are perfectionists. At the very least, we all seem to have perfectionist tendencies. Those of us who have an inclination toward perfection have had to give ourselves a break as literacy coaches. Life is too complicated and this work is varied and demanding. It is absolutely impossible to be perfect.

Even as I write this, the perfectionist in me pipes up and declares, "But you can try!" Yes, we can *try* to be perfect; we can even die trying. Hallie Williamson, a friend and fellow literacy coach, refers to this as "death by perfection" and, unfortunately, her diagnosis is a sound one. Stress is implicated in a long list of ailments: heart disease, stomach disorders, headaches, high cholesterol, high blood pressure, backaches, and mental disorders (Mayo Clinic, 2006; National Institutes of Health, 2002). Sapolsky (1994) explains that stress is a physiological response to danger, much like the stress a zebra might feel when being chased by a lion. He writes,

> A large body of convergent evidence suggests that stress-related diseases emerge, predominantly, out of the fact that we so often activate a psychological system that has evolved for responding to acute physical emergencies, but we turn it on for months on end.... That the stress-response itself can be harmful makes a certain sense when you examine the things that occur in reaction to stress. They are generally shortsighted, inefficient, and penny-wise and dollar-foolish, but they are the sorts of costly things your body has to do to respond effectively in an emergency. If you experience every day as an emergency, you will pay the price. (pp. 7, 14)

We need to take a deep breath and view ourselves the way we want to view teachers. We should give ourselves the same "givens" we have given them. Literacy coaches deserve to be seen by everyone, especially themselves, in the light of some kind assumptions which, in an effort to accelerate our positive growth, I have begun listing. If we look at this list through the lens of perfectionism, it could resemble a list of weak excuses for not making the grade. But, if we look at it through our compassionate lens, we can find some hope on which to rest.

We care. Whatever the mistake, however we are misunderstood, the critical understanding is this: We care immensely about teachers and our work. If we have done something that communicated to teachers that we don't, it was an accident, and they are likely to forgive us. If they won't, then they are wrestling with issues that are far beyond our control. We are going to make mistakes, probably a lot of them—plan for them psychologically. Mistakes are the necessary byproducts of figuring out a job that is completely new to our field. Errors are like the chemical combinations that are failed attempts at developing a medication; each one takes us closer to where we want to be. If we are not making mistakes, we are not taking risks or putting ourselves in learning situations (Johnston, 2004).

We must treat ourselves kindly; we must give ourselves another chance and another and another. We must remind ourselves, and perhaps those who are being less than kind to us, that we are in this job because we care about teachers and we want their work to be more effective, easier, and more joyful. If we trip on the way, we can let our concern for teachers pull us up and set us moving again.

We have already made a difference. Things are getting better. Maybe there is a lot left for us to do, and maybe we are pessimistic. But, in all likelihood, if we have been operating from a respectful stance and have been working from a sound research foundation, things such as instruction, assessment, and the school culture have improved since we joined our schools.

Improvement doesn't have to be tremendous to be significant. Growing just one relationship in some pretty rocky soil is a success, and you need to take a minute to stop and smell the roses you have nurtured. If you do nothing during the first year of your coaching experience but learn the school culture and develop positive, supporting relationships with teachers, you have accomplished much.

Our motives are honest. Again, we may make gross errors and huge blunders, but our motives are sincerely about nurturing teachers and promoting strong instruction. If we hang onto these motives and continue to operate from them, the preponderance of our work will resonate with this truth and teachers will, even if they need a little time, get past our mistakes. Our mistakes often seem big because they can affect a lot of people, but everyone makes them and, if we can forgive others, we should forgive ourselves. In the end, our sincerity will become the hallmark of our work, and our mistakes will be in the shadow of the philosophy that drives us.

So, even if our teachers don't know it yet, we are sincerely interested in helping, and our motives are not self-serving. If our motives haven't been sincere, we can give ourselves a pat on the back right now for being honest with ourselves. Then we can think about how sincere people behave and act as they do. In all likelihood, we will grow to be more sincere. If we practice being who we want to be, then we will grow in that direction. We can celebrate the recognition that we need to change, the focus in a particular direction, and the progress we will make.

We are hard workers. No, this is not enough in and of itself—we can work very hard at something that is completely ineffective. Nevertheless, hard work generally pays dividends, and we certainly aren't going to facilitate change in our schools if we don't invest some serious mental and physical sweat.

We can give ourselves a word of encouragement and think about the things we accomplished that will help our school move in a positive direction. More than likely we have put in many hours of planning. Maybe we have been analyzing data, hauling boxes, organizing a bookroom, developing a long-range vision, and studying research. Hard work, especially when it is also smart, usually brings rewards.

We have another chance tomorrow. Tomorrow is a new day. Although cliché, this statement is apt. Sometimes we just need to divert our attention from our failures until they are less fresh in our minds. We should go home and kiss our spouse, talk to a friend, read a novel, rock a baby, plant a tree, sing a song, write a poem, paint a house...whatever we can enjoy that isn't related to school. Things will be better in the morning. We all know this. We just have to remember it at the point of exhaustion or the climax of frustration.

We need to pull ourselves away and have the faith to do something else in order for that "thing," that dreadful, horrible thing (which, of course, isn't nearly as dreadful or horrible as it seems at the moment) to take care of itself while we are taking care of ourselves.

We learn from our mistakes. Mistakes are good. People actually learn from mistakes. In fact, we won't grow nearly as fast or as far if we do everything perfectly the first time. Mistakes foster reflection, which keeps us thinking, processing, and questioning. Making mistakes makes us think, and learning from our mistakes keeps our brains in shape.

We should conserve the energy we spend beating ourselves up and use it to analyze our situation. Meanwhile, the teachers with whom we have relationships, and even some who are just kind people, are going to be forgiving. Whatever the outcome, we have learned something about ourselves, the teachers, and our work that we can keep in our pocket for later.

We have made it safe for teachers to take risks. We may not realize it but having an "expert" at school can be intimidating to teachers. There may be some who will hesitate to speak up because they are afraid that we will find them wrong.

It is good to make a mess of things every once in a while, good for us and good for teachers. It reminds us of the need for multiple experts in a school and shows the faculty that we aren't afraid to recognize our mistakes and that, afterward, we can rally and move on. Maybe we'll even get to laugh at ourselves, which takes us to an even healthier place and makes us even more approachable.

We exercise patience. Real change is slow. Lasting change does not happen overnight. Although others may pressure us to think and act around the idea that significant changes can happen instantly, literacy coaches know better. Fullan (2001) writes,

> in an era of high-stakes testing in schools and with a sense of urgency to show short-term results, leaders in a culture of change require a quality that all long-term effective leaders have—the capacity to resist a focus on short-term gains at the expense of deeper reform where gains are steady but not necessarily dramatic. (p. 63)

Coaches must have such patience; we must resist the urge to rush an innately slow process. Building learning communities and shaping classroom practice takes time. As Wenger and Snyder (2000) so aptly put it, "You can't tug on a cornstalk to make it grow faster or taller, and you shouldn't yank a marigold out of the ground to see if it has roots" (p. 143). Resisting pressures to expedite change can take its toll on a literacy coach, and we are wise to remind ourselves that research supports what we already know: Change takes time, and this time affords us the opportunity to offset little setbacks with successes. The realities of change serve as padding we can wrap around our blunders, minimizing their negative affect and maximizing our opportunity to learn from them.

We are reflective learners. We are moving forward. When coaches reflect on their professional and personal lives, they see where they have grown and where they still need to grow. As reflective learners, we are all moving along this giant continuum of growth in the direction of being better. Better at our jobs, better at relating to other people, better at taking care of ourselves, better at forgiving ourselves, better at parenting, better at writing....

We are each getting better in the areas critical to our work and personal lives, and that is important. Whether we are progressing quickly or taking our time, forward is forward, and we deserve to have our progress noted, especially by ourselves. It doesn't matter where we started, whether it was ahead of or behind someone else. It doesn't matter how far we have to go. What matters is that we are growing and, while we may stumble periodically, we are consistently becoming better people, whatever that means for each of us, and this is significant, important work.

How Do We Take Care of Ourselves?

So, how exactly are we going to take care of ourselves in this work? Some schools can act as black holes of need and once we are sucked into them, it is virtually impossible to pull ourselves back out. For example, once we establish that we are willing to put in 30 extra hours a week or spend our own money to build classroom libraries, that type of personal sacrifice will always be expected. Our work culture in the United States, especially in education, can make us feel as if we aren't committed to our jobs if we advocate for ourselves at all. We shouldn't readily accept this idea; if we don't advocate for ourselves, we will not be able to survive in the position long enough to advocate for teachers. Following are several specific ways we can take care of ourselves in our work as literacy coaches:

We can create our own environments. I have already discussed this at length in chapter 2, but it bears repeating in this context. The decisions a coach makes early in his work will establish his philosophy of coaching and will put him in a position to preserve or to sacrifice himself. We must proceed with caution and think deeply about the choices we are making.

During my first year as literacy coach, I really struggled with keeping the boundaries between home and school distinct. For example, I was nursing my son, who was just a few months old at the time, and my husband came to school every day at lunchtime. I sat in the car with them and nursed my son during the 30 minutes I took for lunch. My husband would bring my lunch and I would eat while the baby ate. We would talk about matters other than school, and often he would read aloud to me.

This daily ritual was something I discussed with the principal of the school and established before I took the position. After I was offered the position, I explained that I wanted to nurse my son in the middle of the day each day and that my husband would be available to bring the baby to me. My new principal agreed. I have a friend who is a literacy coach who has been following this same routine with her son for a couple of years now. Other principals may not be as agreeable, but our early days as a literacy coach are the time to determine just how flexible they are.

While these daily repasts obviously met the nutritional needs of my son, they also filled my psychological needs in powerful ways. They softened that very difficult first year away from my son and in a demanding position, and they reminded me daily that there was a big world beyond the school walls.

We can leave some margins in our work lives. We don't have to wear our schedules so tightly that we can't breathe. If we work in a particular classroom next week rather than this week, the world will not end, and we will probably do a better job. Usually, when I make mistakes in my work, it is because I've overscheduled myself or let other people overschedule me.

Like me, most coaches need practice saying "no." We can only keep so many plates spinning before one drops, and that will bring with it a different kind of a stress and a fair amount of clean up. We can schedule some time between classes, some early morning time to focus, and some late afternoon time to reflect. All of these buffers between activities keep us sane in our work and possibly add years to our lives.

We can plan for our own professional growth. I always feel guilty when I spend time attending to my professional growth, because it usually takes me away from the school. In fact, some of the best professional learning I have participated in has taken me away from the school for a whole week at a time. I didn't attend any off-site professional learning sessions during my first two years as a coach. I did attend a couple of day-long workshops, but I took teachers with me.

While coaches also learn when they participate in professional learning with teachers, this does not count as professional learning for literacy coaches. If a coach attends professional learning with teachers, he will want to support their reflection. He will want to push conversations and pay attention to teacher responses to the learning events. Because he supports teachers' reflection on what they have learned, the coach won't have sufficient time to process what he has learned.

I am glad to participate in professional learning with teachers; I think most coaches are. However, it is fatiguing, and it can keep us from our own reflection. The teachers get more personal growth out of professional learning when they are supported. If we want to attend professional learning for our own growth, we need to go alone or with other coaches. It is not at all unreasonable to push for the time to grow ourselves.

We can take care of our bodies. This is one of the biggest challenges in literacy coaching. I suspect that the vast majority of new literacy coaches have become less healthy since they began coaching. Most will tell you that they don't sleep as well, because they are often awake in the middle of the night thinking about an idea, trying to solve a problem, or lamenting a mistake. They will probably say that their eating habits have gotten worse, because they are continually on the run with little time to plan, shop for, or pack thoughtful meals and snacks.

There have been many days when I have been working for hours, only to realize that I haven't had anything to drink the entire day or that it is 2:00 p.m. and I never ate lunch. I will sit for five hours straight entering assessment data into my computer and not even pause to stretch. Even as I sit here writing about how literacy coaches need to take care of themselves, I realize that I have not moved from this spot in front of my computer for seven hours.

We need to eat. We need to drink. (Making merry is the next clichéd step, and I don't think it would hurt us.) We need to stretch and step outside. We should give our bodies a little support and a little break. Burning ourselves out at work is not going to make anyone a better reading teacher. Furthermore, real change is slow, so we can take the time in our schedule to take a deep breath every now and then. It's OK to take care of ourselves.

We can go home. As I am writing this on a Sunday morning, my 2-year-old is playing at my feet. He moves from his wooden blocks to the yellow highlighter and blank paper that I have put on the coffee table for him to "write his name." I am distracted by my writing, and he wants my attention. He comes over to me and my laptop, closes the screen, and furrows his brow as he instructs me, "Play with that tomorrow, Mommy. Play with that tomorrow."

All of the teachers with whom we work should have something at home that is more important to them than their profession and so should we. If we don't, we need to leave school and find a meaningful distraction. We can take a walk, take an art class, or write a poem. We can write about work if we have to, but we need to get away from the school environment. Leaving school to renew ourselves will help us perform our jobs better when we return. This is the whole truth and nothing but; we are not machines.

We can practice positive habits. The key word here is *practice*. We need to decide what behaviors we want to adopt, and then we need to practice them like we would practice the piano or tennis. Perhaps we should say, "rent to own" them. Rent the behaviors until they are truly yours. I am still trying to own positive patterns of thinking, and, after paying much emotional and intellectual currency, I am beginning to feel confident that I will someday own them.

Resisting negativity is a common challenge. One of my twins was struggling with his schoolwork and was feeling really down about himself. I had a conference with his teacher because I was concerned that she was not encouraging him enough at school. She was very open to my thoughts on the matter and said that she would do the "bean thing" with Christopher the next day. I asked her what the bean thing was, and she described it as a way to develop a habit of being positive with a child.

A teacher puts 10 beans in one pocket. Every time she says something positive to the child in question she moves a bean over to the other pocket. If the teacher says something corrective or negative, she moves a bean back to the original pocket. The goal is to move all the beans from the first pocket to the second pocket by the end of the day.

This pocket procedure is also a clever way to systematically develop the habits we covet. If we want to be more positive about ourselves, we can put some marbles in a pocket and see how troublesome it is to get them moved over to another pocket by the end of the day. (Of course, we also have to get past being down on ourselves if we weren't able to get all the marbles moved over.) If we try this for a few days, the habit will become automatic. Whatever positive habit we want to adopt, we can give ourselves a tangible system for establishing it. Whether it is beans in our pockets or rubber bands on our wrist, we can claim the habits we wish we had without losing all our marbles.

We can recognize our limitations. Literacy coaches who think they know pretty much everything about literacy instruction in an elementary school set themselves up for a difficult lesson. Coaches who realize that they don't know everything about literacy should make this self-awareness public knowledge. Wheatley (2002) writes, "We weren't trained to admit we don't know. Most of us were taught to sound certain and confident, to state our opinion as if it were true. We haven't been rewarded for being confused. Or for asking more questions rather than giving quick answers" (p. 34).

In the work of change, we all (i.e., teachers, administrators, literacy coaches) must take the time to let ourselves be confused. There is no "Aha!" moment without first having a problem. We must bury ourselves in the confusion because only then will we have the opportunity to dig our way out. And the digging is just as important as eventually seeing the light, because digging builds muscle and develops transferable skills.

We can let go of some of the responsibility. We can't "own all the problems" (Toll, 2005, p. 134). We cannot take responsibility for all the failures within our schools any more than we can take responsibility for all the successes. There are a million variables that influence change within schools. Ineffective administrators can hobble coaches' efforts. Material resources are required to implement most instructional changes. Coaches need time with teachers, and that is often unavailable. Teachers themselves have more ownership and more responsibility in their own learning, and at some point we have to let them carry some of the weight of the change.

For some reason, we will gladly don the suit of responsibility when instructional change has been unsuccessful, but when change moves forward we are a lot less likely to try on any celebration. For many of us, we vehemently lay claim to the areas where instructional progress stagnates in our schools while we robustly decline recognizing our roles in the undertakings that are successful.

We can build a support system under ourselves. This support system doesn't have to include 100 people. Even having just one person who can encourage us will make a difference. During my first year as a coach, Peggy Terrell acted as a scaffold for me. Peggy is a language arts consultant who came to our school and consulted with us and me personally about our language arts work. I was new to the area and did not have a network of friends or family to support me. Peggy was my port in the storm. If I was discouraged or my energy was flagging, she would shore me up, and I would be able to keep going until her next visit. I also developed alliances with the few other coaches I knew. One in particular became someone with whom I could commiserate or celebrate and to whom I could speak in confidence.

We can plan nurturing transitions to and from work. If, on any given day, we avoid being swallowed by our jobs, we have done a good day's work. The challenge isn't always physical. Sometimes the weight of coaching can follow us home, even if we have left all physical evidence of work back at school. We can physically leave the school yet our brains remain at our desk preparing written feedback for a teacher. This means, of course, that we are distracted in our home lives and that our connections with our families are hindered. Shaky family connections provide less opportunity for us to renew, which means we return to work dragging our emotional debt.

I have found that it helps to set up some routines to support my transitions between home and work. If we can find something engaging enough to help us forget about work *and* home for just a few minutes, we will have a gentler transition from one environment to the other.

For example, I am learning to play the piano. If I take 15 minutes at the piano to support the return to my "home atmosphere," then I won't burn up upon reentry. Playing the piano takes every ounce of my concentration, which means I have no mental space to think about work or home. It is a bridge between the two worlds, a neutral space for my brain to take a deep "breath."

Another transitional ritual I have in place, one which I am dedicated to practicing, involves reading or listening to a poem every morning. I have registered to receive a poem each day from Writer's Almanac (http://writersalmanac.publicradio.org/). Each morning when I arrive at school, I have a poem waiting for me. Even if I have 300 e-mails in my inbox and they are all flagged urgent, I read the poem first. The poems are rarely about education so they let me start my day in a neutral mental space. I print out the poems that move me and put them into a notebook. Through this process, I have assembled a personal poetry anthology and have given myself a mental vitamin to jump-start each day.

This ritual elevates my day, and each morning that I practice it, regardless of the prior day's disasters, it reliably formalizes the start of a new morning. Every morning, it is like cleaning the glass through which I look at my day.

Souvenirs

Dillard (1989) says, "How we spend our days is, of course, how we spend our lives" (p. 32). As coaches, we spend most of our days, and hence, most of our lives at school. It is worth our time to plan, psychologically and on paper, in order to enjoy the efforts that fill our days. Such self-preservation requires that we consciously engage strategies that systematically prevent us from doing the very thing that has historically indicated commitment in the field of education: sacrifice ourselves. However, there is no crime in treating ourselves kindly, and the oxygen masks we slip on ourselves will help us support the teachers in our schools in their critical efforts to take a deep breath.

The People:
Building Relationships

CHAPTER 4

The Organism and the Organization: Working With Individuals and Groups

"[C]ommunity ties are not loosening. They've just moved into the workplace."
Richard Reeves, *Happy Mondays: Putting the Pleasure Back Into Work,*
2001, p. 118

I once had a conversation with a professional portrait photographer who told me that taking portraits is less about cameras, equipment, and technique and more about working with people. A portrait photographer has to know how to engage people so they will relax in front of the camera. Photographers' technical skills can be weak, but if their "people skills" are strong, they are likely to get appealing pictures. However, if photographers have strong technical skills but poor people skills, then their portraits are likely to be boring.

Similarly, literacy coaching is 25% energy, 25% passion, 25% content knowledge, 25% organization, and 100% relationshipping. I know the math and the grammar are wrong, but the idea is sound. None of the energy, the passion, the expertise, or the organizational skills we bring to literacy coaching will have any effect on our schools if we can't relate to the teachers. Ours is a people profession, and I can have the IQ (intelligence quotient) of a genius yet fail miserably if I don't take the time to develop relationships.

Goleman (1995) explores the relationship between IQ and success, and concludes that emotional intelligence is as important, if not more important, that IQ. He argues that emotional illiteracy can be debilitating for leaders, and he gives them guidance in supporting their employees emotionally. Similarly, Hogan, Raskin, and Fazzini (1990) explored three types of mistakes made by principals in communicating with staff. They found that most mistakes were associated with principals who had poor relationship skills. The most common mistake was that they did not demonstrate trust or care, two related characteristics.

These leadership mistakes are symptomatic of a detached leader who doesn't have the time, skill, or inclination to know her faculty. Some literacy coaches try to work similarly. When they are faced with the challenges of facilitating change in a school, they try to work *around* teachers rather than *with* them. This, quite obviously, is a losing proposition. The school loses time, energy, and money, while the children lose instruction. Although much of the role of a literacy coach hinges on expertise and experience, the bedrock of effective coaching is sturdy relationships with teachers. These, of course, develop over time as we demonstrate consistently that we are knowledgeable, sincere, trustworthy, respectful, and committed.

Some people suggest that schools should be more like businesses (e.g., Chubb & Moe, 1990). However, I believe educators are a cross between pediatricians and child psychologists. A portion of our work is largely predictable because of the research base that supports it. The other part of our work revolves around personalities and self-concepts, and these things are less predictable. Teachers are charged with making children intellectually healthy, and this isn't just a matter of writing a prescription.

The intellectual–psychological balance of growth is necessary for all of us. We have to protect and nurture the well-being of teachers within our school because the emotional places in which teachers exist collectively form the school culture. We have to make room for teachers to feel and be at school so, in giving them permission to be both intellectually and emotionally awake in their work, the children whom they teach will have the benefit of learning from their example. In fact, psychological state is highly correlated with teacher effectiveness in implementing the strategies they learn in professional learning settings (Hopkins, 1990).

We do not work with teachers in spite of their moods and their personality differences. We work with them to support them as they channel their reflective and emotional lives into their work and as they contribute to the mosaic of personalities that forms the school's emotional core. The relationships we have with the faculty in our school will evolve and change over time, just like every other relationship we have.

The Bay Area School Reform Collaborative (BASRC) has developed a coaching procedure that moves through five stages. "Relationship Building" is a stage in itself that validates the critical initial work of building trust:

> At first the balance weighs more heavily toward a facilitative approach as the coach and the school client learn to work with each other and build relationships. As productive relationships develop, the coach is better positioned to be more of an advocate and is better able to encourage the use of inquiry to close the achievement gap. (Barr, Simmons, & Zarrow, 2003, p. 21)

Our relationships with teachers will also cycle through times of strength and times when the connections between us and a particular teacher seem a little tenuous. This is normal. It is the extremes of this cycle that we must work to avoid. Our relationships with teachers can be compromised to the point that it is impossible to recover as a coach. A teacher feeling a bit out of touch with us is less serious than a teacher feeling betrayed. At the other extreme, we can get so close to one or a few teachers that we alienate others. The impact of these two extremes goes beyond the teacher directly affected; word spreads through the school, and our pillars of support become shaky beneath us. Nobody else really cares too much if a teacher feels a little out of touch with us; however, everyone will listen to a teacher who feels betrayed or excluded.

Building a learning community in a school can be as challenging as—perhaps even more challenging than—developing a classroom community. Adults are complicated. Personality conflicts inevitably arise, and there may be histories of conflict that started in our schools long before we ever entered the building. By valuing a sense of professionalism and by respecting teachers, even the ones that nearly everyone dislikes, we communicate that caring is a priority. Robb (2000) writes,

Closed minds, like closed doors, often take time to rattle and unlock. My job was to put aside personal frustrations, find common ground, and build enough trust between me and these teachers so that we could engage in meaningful dialogue. Time, patience, a nonthreatening stance, and inviting them to share teaching strategies enabled relationships to develop. Only then could coaching begin. (p. 76)

This "people work" that paves the way for intellectual work requires that coaches exercise sense beyond books. Care will deliver your message to rich soil and predispose your listeners to give these new ideas room to grow. Jensen (2004) speaks to the role relationships play in being human:

Why do you care about them?

Because I'm human.

Why does being human imply you should care?

Because a human being is not simply an ego structure in a sack of skin. Human beings, and this is true for all beings, are the relationships they share. My health—emotional, physical, moral—is inextricably intertwined with the quality of these relationships, whether I acknowledge the relationships or not. (pp. 105–106)

When we begin to recognize teachers as the people they are around and beyond and behind teaching, then our coaching changes. I work with a second-grade teacher who had a son who died suddenly when he was 2 years old. The day I learned of it, I took this information home with me and held my son, who was 9 months old. My coaching of the teacher changed as my understanding of her became deeper. And as the stories of all the teachers with whom I work trickle out and as I honor those as part of who they are as teachers and human beings, my coaching becomes more human, too, and not surprisingly, more effective. Ours is a people profession, and if we make room for teachers to be human beings in their work, then they are in a better place to do the same for children.

Building Relationships

Building relationships is largely a matter of respect and time. However, following I also provide a few common sense suggestions that may be helpful to consider as we forge ahead in getting to know our teachers and letting them get to know us.

About Listening

If we watch and listen to teachers more than we talk to them, we will find that they usually know what their important projects need to be. They know what element of the instructional framework they need to study; perhaps we know the books to suggest. We are ready with a copy of *Wondrous Words: Writers and Writing in the Elementary Classroom* (Ray, 1999) when a teacher says, "I need to work on my writing instruction. Can you recommend something for me to read?" Of course, we have fostered an environment where it is safe to say, "I need help with writer's workshop." The teacher is confident that we won't respond negatively. Teachers know that we appreciate their personal and instructional strengths, and with that knowledge they are comfortable talking with us about their goals for the literacy instruction in their classrooms.

When I was working at RESA, I dealt with 15 different school systems and within most of those, I worked with several schools. One of my jobs was to communicate with the school or district leadership in order to plan professional learning for them. I would listen to them describe their work and their goals, and inevitably, when I returned to my office to plan, I would find gaps in my information. I learned from a colleague that I needed to listen more systematically, and I intentionally changed the way I listened in those contexts.

So, as my colleague had suggested, after a few minutes of listening, I repeated, expanded, and clarified. I would say, "This is what I hear you saying...." and then I would try to restate in my own words what the person had said. I would elaborate on various parts and ask questions to get clarification. Then the person would continue talking and the process would start again. Obviously, this is a very slow way to conduct a conversation and, if taken to an extreme, can become ridiculous. However, if used sensibly, I think this process is more effective and less time-consuming than having to retrace our steps to clarify our misunderstandings.

The aforementioned procedure is relatively simple; however, listening is not as simple as it seems. Few of us are truly skilled listeners. In *The Seven Habits of Highly Effective People: Powerful Lessons in*

Personal Change, Covey (1989) describes five levels of listening: (1) ignoring, (2) pretending, (3) selective listening, (4) attentive listening, and (5) empathic listening (p. 240). I have modified these levels by representing them in the following hierarchy of statements:

1. I don't care.
2. I'm pretending to care.
3. I care about some of what you are saying.
4. I care about everything you are saying.
5. I care about you and everything you are saying.

You've probably heard the sage advice that you should listen more than you speak. This is considerably easier when you care. Perhaps our ability to listen is directly related to our level of care about the person doing the talking. This statement may be a stretch, but at least in some situations I think it is true. Furthermore, when we listen to teachers we grow to care for them more. It is, I think, impossible to separate listening from caring, just as it is impossible to separate learning to read from learning to write. Work in one of these areas will affect both, and growth in either area will yield fruit in the other.

Listening is not something that comes easily to me or that I think I do well. I am continually working on this. Often, when I talk to teachers, I try to complete their sentences rather than wait for them to finish. Other times, I take the first thing a teacher says and begin to process it, turning it over in my head and beginning to problem solve. All the while, the teacher is still sharing important background information, and I haven't heard anything past the first statement. Fullan (2001) says, "Effective leaders listen attentively—you can almost hear them listening" (pp. 123–124). I still struggle with being effective in this area.

Fortunately, listening skills can be learned. If we find someone who we know to be a good listener, we can learn from him. I can say to myself, "This is what I see good listeners doing, so if I want to be a good listener, I need to do that, too." We have to *act* like listeners if we want to develop listening skills. The word *act* may be a little unsettling, but I mean it only in the way we teach beginning readers to act like experienced readers. If I actually practice these techniques, I am likely to adopt at least some of these listening strategies.

About Talking

If we are listening, it means that someone is talking to us, and this kind of listening carries with it a certain responsibility. A literacy coach can lose her credibility with teachers instantly by violating their confidences. Confidentiality isn't limited to the conversations we have with teachers but includes what we see when we visit a classroom. The relationship between confidentiality and trust is a direct and simple one. However, living up to it isn't always simple. Nevertheless, skills of discretion are essential to our work and certainly worth developing.

If we are working in teachers' classrooms, it is as if we are guests in their homes. If I am invited into someone's home for dinner, and I notice dust on the furniture, I need to reserve judgment, and I certainly shouldn't go out and talk to people about it. More important, if I am noticing dust on the furniture when someone has taken the time to cook for me, there is a bigger, systemic problem that is about me. If I can't give people the benefit of the doubt, then I better keep my opinions to myself.

Perhaps I think that I can talk with a particular teacher about another teacher's classroom. Maybe I need to unload a bit. Maybe I really do want some support in looking for ways to help the teacher. Perhaps my motives for talking with a teacher about another teacher are pure. It is probably still inappropriate.

Even if the person to whom I speak doesn't tell anyone else (and he probably will), even if it is a professional conversation (and it's probably not), and even if he is my best friend (and he probably shouldn't be), I am demonstrating that I am untrustworthy. Furthermore, on some level, however small, the person to whom I am speaking is thinking to himself, "If she'll talk about so-and-so, she'll talk about me," and his concerns will be justified.

I tend to take this not-talking-about-teachers thing to an extreme on a couple of levels. First, I don't even like to talk *positively* about teachers to other teachers. I try to limit holding a teacher up as a model unless I can connect two teachers who can benefit each other. I have found that singling out teachers for sound practices can be divisive, and that it often makes the teacher being praised uncomfortable. Teachers just don't like to be singled out as positive or negative examples. Furthermore, praise can become a form of extrinsic reward that overshadows more valuable intrinsic rewards. There is a muddy threshold between giving appropriate positive feedback and overloading with praise. Crossing this line, intentionally or inadvertently, can put a literacy coach in a position of power, and this is unsafe territory if solid relationships are going to develop.

To date, the times I have used the work of any teacher as an example for others are so few that I can only think of one right now. Furthermore, in this one instance where I pointed out a teacher's strengths, hers was highlighted as one example out of a whole pool of quality work that was also recognized. I thought long and hard before I did it and, even now, I'm still not sure it was wise. Presently, I am organizing peer-coaching opportunities for teachers. However, this is strategic, and every teacher who has been at our school long enough to develop some deep understandings around literacy will eventually have the opportunity to be visited by colleagues.

I have another self-imposed rule of extreme silence: I won't let teachers talk negatively about other teachers to me. In talking about conversation skills, Scott says, "You get what you tolerate" (2002, p. 59), and I believe this to be true. Not only this, but if we establish our conversation comfort zones with just one teacher, if we have this uncomfortable conversation one time, we probably won't have to have it again. Word of our philosophy will spread to every other teacher in the building. This is good gossip, and it helps teachers begin to trust us. If we do have to have this conversation more than once, it will be much easier because by then we will have observed the benefits of candidly articulating our philosophy.

This can be difficult. I have had to say more than once, "I'm not comfortable with this conversation." Teachers have come to me to unload about colleagues, and I respect their need for this, and oftentimes I understand. However, if their tone is hurtful or angry, I just can't offer a listening ear. If the conversation can truly stay professional, and occasionally it can, then I am able to offer professional advice about the situation. This can happen only when the teacher with whom I am talking and I are able to assume that the teacher in question has the best of intentions.

However, conversations about colleagues that are more related to gossip are something I am vigilant about suppressing in my presence. Even a conversation that begins professionally can quickly slip into something inappropriate. If a teacher regularly starts sentences with "I don't mean to be ugly but..." or "I don't want to be unprofessional but...," then I will interrupt, smile, and say, "Then don't." This response is a bit extreme and will probably only be necessary if there is a chronic problem. However, I have had to do this, and it has not hurt me to come out strongly in favor of speaking respectfully about colleagues.

The issue of supporting gossip is worth taking a step further. We implicitly support gossip by letting it happen in our presence, even if we are not participating. The message I want to clearly communicate to teachers is that I won't let teachers talk about other teachers in my presence. I will address it directly, leave the room, or close my door. The subtext for teachers is, "If she won't let me talk about so-and-so around her, then she won't let anybody else talk about me." This makes me a safe place to which teachers can go to be honest and seek encouragement.

I have a son with Attention Deficit Hyperactivity Disorder (ADHD), and he went to a psychologist for a battery of tests before he was diagnosed. Later, I met with the doctor to talk about the results. We conversed for about an hour, and he answered my questions thoroughly. I trusted him and, by the end of the session, we seemed to have built a rapport. On the way out we began making small talk, and somehow he got on the subject of funny responses he had received from patients when giving IQ tests. At first I thought it was entertaining, but as the examples continued, I grew increasingly uncomfortable, although I couldn't pinpoint why.

Later, after reflecting on the conversation with my husband, I came to understand: It was simply unprofessional for the doctor to talk about his patients this way, even if they remained anonymous. He exhibited a gross lack of respect for his patients as people, which naturally led me to question his interactions with my son. Did he respect or appreciate the complexity of the challenges we were facing? Did he understand the impact ADHD had had on our family and, more important, did he really care?

If he would talk about patients with me, how did I know that my son wouldn't come up at a dinner party somewhere? What if my son had done something really unusual during testing, or what if he had given some bizarre or humorous answer to a question; would his testing behavior later become fodder for small talk? This doctor was suddenly unsafe for us, and I found myself taking a protective stance.

My point is literacy coaches can't be too careful about what they say. We need to err on the side of caution and keep our consciences clean, because mistakes in this arena can result in injuries that have long recovery times or are permanent. No literacy coach needs the kind of setback in her work that a violation of confidence can bring with it. If relationship building is the most critical part of our work (and it is), then honoring confidences is the most critical part of building relationships.

It is certainly true that on most staffs there are teachers who are more difficult to work with than others. Every now and then we will have the opportunity to work with one of these teachers—someone who possibly is combative, unprofessional, immature, or even vindictive. Nevertheless, we can't climb on board the school gossip train, even if our conversation is disguised as a professional one. Even if a teacher is difficult, we shouldn't behave unprofessionally. If we can focus our energy on coaching instruction rather than on applying emotional first aid and exercising emergency interventions in an effort to save our credibility, teachers and students will benefit.

About Time

If relationship development rests in learning to communicate, then time is the critical element in doing so. Time is the fuel on which relationships run. It is difficult, if not impossible, to have a relationship with someone without spending time with him. This year I have benefited from my school district's hiring of instructional coaches for every school and providing them with professional learning. We have assembled regularly for a variety of district-provided opportunities to grow professionally and to develop our learning community. In fact, I have spent three full weeks out of classrooms this year in intense study with these coaches.

The benefits of this training are obvious. However, the weekly and the week-long meetings took their toll on my relationships with the teachers in our school. I simply felt out-of-touch. If a relationship is "hardy," it will survive the push and pull of time spent apart. However, literacy coaches should be judicious about spending time away from their schools, especially during their earliest efforts to build relationships.

Literacy coaches continually make choices about where to put their time and energy. Given that our time is not unlimited and that we want to spend most of it in direct support of teachers, it helps to have some criteria for making decisions. Generally, I ask myself a few questions.

- Can I get satisfactory results more quickly by completing the task in a different way?

- Is the amount of payback for this task equal to or greater than the amount of time I will spend doing it?

- Will anything be compromised if I decide to wait on this?

- Do I have all the information I need to do this task well?

- Is there someone who can give me a new perspective on this task? Do I know someone with strength in the area in which I am working?

- Is there someone who can share this task with me (i.e., volunteers, the school secretary, a student)?

- How does this work affect instruction, the school culture, or both? If it doesn't, why do I need to do it? If it does, is the amount of benefit worth the amount of time it takes to do the task?

- Based on my hourly rate, is the school district getting good value for my work if I spend my time on this project?

Most of these are common sense questions that any book on time management would address. The challenge is not in understanding the questions, but rather in taking the time to ask them in the barrage of reports, requests, and "fires" to which we must attend. Making wise choices about which tasks we allow to claim our time will give us more time with teachers to develop relationships and address instructional goals. As with many of the issues I discuss in this book, I find it much easier to write about time management than to manage my time, and sometimes I am not sure if I have made wise choices.

For example, I have been working with a new teacher. She is intelligent, hardworking, intuitive, and dedicated. If I suggest she try something, she does so right away and sticks with it until it works for her. If I set up a time for her to watch instruction in someone else's room, she will have the new routine or method established in her room in a week.

Recently I spent an entire week in her classroom modeling guided reading. As part of the modeling, I wanted to work through all the management issues associated with guided reading. This meant that I needed to set up a record-keeping system for guided reading lessons, a way to organize the materials for each group, a way to manage running records, and so forth. I spent three hours putting all this together for her. It involved making copies, organizing notebooks, gathering materials, setting up folders, and such. I was not sure this was good use of my time, particularly when I considered that she might want to change the system completely to meet her taste and style.

However, the Monday following my week in the classroom, my administrator happened to be in her classroom, unaware that it was her first day to "fly solo" with guided reading. This teacher implemented with amazing competence all the elements of guided reading. She managed independent groups, took a running record, and kept documentation of her teaching points. A few days later, I went into her room to watch guided reading and then decided that the few hours setting up guided reading for her were well spent. Basically, sometimes the most valuable use of our time is counterintuitive, and it involves risk and faith to follow our instincts.

I worked through a similar struggle as I was developing relationships with teachers. When I first started working as a literacy coach I knew that relationship building would be an important part of my work. For the first year, I gave any teacher who needed it my immediate attention. If I was working on something in my office, maybe studying curriculum materials or planning my schedule, I would stop immediately if a teacher needed me. I always—if it was in my power to do so—dropped whatever I was doing to talk with a teacher.

In the beginning, the discussions were always professional or dealt with some particular instructional issue. Eventually teachers began to talk about personal issues that were so heavy on their minds that they needed to unload them in order to come back to school psychologically. I specifically remember the first time this happened and the satisfaction I felt in knowing the teacher felt safe with me. Gradually, teachers shared bad days, successes, struggles, and ideas, and by being relatively available for them, I hoped to communicate that I was there to be of service.

At times I questioned this choice. Sometimes the conversations felt like chitchat; sometimes they were chitchat. However, in the end, the decision to give teachers my attention any time I could proved to help develop a solid base for our relationships. I have held onto this practice whenever I have been able. For the most part, the only time I tell a teacher that I can't talk with her is when I am already talking with another teacher or when I am scheduled to be somewhere else. Even then, I try to set up another time to get together. Scott (2002) writes,

> If the conversation stops, all of the possibilities for the relationship become smaller and all of the possibilities for the individuals in the relationship

become smaller, until one day we overhear ourselves in midsentence, making *ourselves* smaller in every encounter, behaving as if we are just the space around our shoes, engaged in yet another three-minute conversation so empty of meaning it crackles. (p. 6)

The lines of communication between teachers and coaches must stay open, and this requires focused effort. Relationships are built on conversations and connections. The stronger the conversations and the deeper the connections, the more meaningful the work becomes. Meaningful work leads to lasting change and facilitates an atmosphere of reflection.

Assuming Goodwill

"Teachers aren't broken." Peg Gwyther, a consultant who coaches coaches, was the first person I heard make this statement. Since then I have read it in a number of places. Teachers aren't broken; coaches don't need to fix anyone. Barkley and Bianco (2005) speak to this, "Coaching is not about fixing someone. No one is broken, and no one needs fixing. It's not about giving advice, providing 'constructive criticism,' making judgments, or providing an opinion. Coaching is a relationship..." (p. 4).

In most cases, coaches are hired because someone with the authority to hire them believes that the school in which they are placed needs to improve. While all schools can improve, there is a continuum of need. Some schools manifest broad needs and are on the verge of collapse, while other schools are largely successful, having only pockets of children who are not responding to the current instruction.

Regardless of the severity of the need, it seems that the blame for causing it and the responsibility for correcting it often falls on teachers. Because we have spent years teaching reading, literacy coaches should know that teachers have the most difficult jobs in the school. Their jobs are the most constant, the most confining, the most scrutinized, and the most critical. Nevertheless, teachers remain committed to their students as well as their own professional growth. Research demonstrates that "teachers are wonderful learners. Nearly all teachers can acquire new skills that 'fine tune' their competence" (Joyce & Showers, 1980, p. 379).

Early in my work as a coach I decided to operate from a few premises. These have been my "givens" with teachers as I have worked with them. I work hard to ensure that these ideas are communicated to teachers.

- Teachers want to be better at their jobs.
- Teachers want all of their students to be broadly literate.
- Teachers care about children.
- Teachers want to learn.
- Teachers want to teach.
- Teachers have the most difficult jobs in education.
- Teachers have the most important jobs in education.
- Teachers have the least respected jobs in a field that earns little respect.
- Teachers know the most about their children.
- Teachers want to be part of a larger learning community.
- Teachers are hard workers.
- Teachers are intelligent.
- Teachers are strong.
- Teachers are competent.
- Teachers want to do what is best for their students.
- Teachers want to know how to improve their instruction.
- Teachers can teach each other.
- Teachers have the right, the expertise, and the insight to play a critical role in decision making regarding curriculum, professional learning, assessment, and instruction.

Assuming goodwill shouldn't be limited to teachers and schools. Once we begin to practice this habit of thought, we will find it an easier and more joyful way to live our lives. I can assume goodwill of my mailperson, my chiropractor, my dearest friend, and most especially, my mate. Rarely is there any harm in assuming goodwill; if we are wrong, we probably don't lose anything by not knowing. If we are right, we have eliminated stress and have added years to our lives.

If we become people who assume the best of others, then life becomes less emotionally congested. If we become literacy coaches who assume the best of teachers, the thorny underbrush of schoolwork begins to die back. Then we can work with teachers unfettered. Much of the time, they will know what they need to work on, and if we are fortunate, they will let us help them.

What's Wrong With Being Right

The assumption of goodwill goes beyond simply believing that everyone is operating from only the purest of motives; it is a matter of giving people room to be authentic. This means operating from the stand that they aren't necessarily wrong, and you aren't necessarily right. McAndrew (2005) says, "Even if you disagree, please don't make me wrong" (p. 115). We manage "agreeing to disagree" successfully by recognizing our fallibility within a professional world that is expansive. We manage by holding tight to our decision to consider teachers as people first and as teachers second. It is interesting to note that when we are not presenting ourselves as the one who is right, teachers are more likely to hear and consider what we are saying.

The truth in the field of literacy instruction is absolute in only a few places. These patches of precision are small islands in a rushing river of literacy research. As we travel down this river, we must be careful what we cling to as absolute truth, because we will have to retrace our steps when the branch breaks. For example, Scott (2002) states,

> So, anyone who comes across as believing that they own the entire, nonnegotiable truth about a particular topic might as well forget about having a fierce conversation. They've struck out before the game began. Become a master at telling the 'truth,' as best you can, while acknowledging that others may have very different truths that are just as valid as yours. (p. 270)

In the context of schools and literacy instruction, we can't wear "right" like a uniform, which allows no room for individuality or freedom of expression. Right must be more like a favorite sweater. So yours is green and mine is blue—does that make mine better? Tomorrow one of us may change and come to school in a different sweater. Perhaps then we will match. Perhaps we won't. Regardless, yours is yours and mine is mine and the difference in the two is fodder for our conversations and a point of contact for our growing relationship.

Souvenirs

Coaching requires caring honestly, intelligently, and equitably. We cannot be effective in our roles if we are neglectful of the multidimensional features of human nature. Nor can we support teachers in nurturing their highest selves without appreciating them holistically. Their willingness to let us support their growth is directly related to their sense of emotional safety, just as our ability to smile naturally in front of a camera is directly related to the sense of ease the photographer manages to instill in us. In a coaching context, a teacher's professional growth, like capturing a compelling likeness in a portrait, is largely the result of intangible human connections.

CHAPTER 5

Taking Risks: The Necessary Discomforts of Change

"Hadn't I, always, but ever and ever, thought that life was just one great risk for the living?"
Maya Angelou, *I Know Why the Caged Bird Sings*, 1983, p. 179

Our teaching and coaching aren't just about initiating change or seeing it come to fruition. Change is primarily about the difficult space in between—the dense process stretched long between beginning and ending points. The norm then becomes disequilibrium so the tension around change becomes hopeful at best and familiar at least. This disequilibrium rests in the slowness and the enormity of significant change, or "deep change" as I refer to it in the remainder of the chapter, but we have to become comfortable with being stretched ourselves and helping others stretch in the process.

Change Is Slow

Deep change takes a long time. For example, as I mentioned, I have been taking piano lessons. Playing the piano is difficult for me, and my progress is torturously slow. If I think about how long it is going to take me to really learn to play the piano, I want to cry, quit, or both. However, my teacher has encouraged me and I have learned to enjoy my present level of skill, however minimal it is. The pieces I play are simple, but I practice "Twinkle, Twinkle Little Star" as if I were preparing for a concert in Carnegie Hall in New York. I look forward to sitting at the piano after a day of work and measuring out a few songs—musical notes that I can follow home like a trail of bread crumbs.

I have to relish my simple songs as if they are an end in and of themselves, because it will be a long time before I can play anything of any real significance, and I will never reach a point where I have learned all there is to know about music. Any genuine growth or change is analogous to piano lessons; we have to be in love with the process, or we won't have the longevity it requires to see any significant product. While I know that I will be playing songs akin to "Twinkle, Twinkle Little Star" for a while, there are points throughout any extended period of learning at which we realize that we have progressed. Eventually, we will reach a point that when someone asks if anyone plays the piano, we feel comfortable responding "I do." Even if the fit is a little loose initially, we begin to think of the change as part of who we are.

Change Is Enormous

Change isn't just slow; it is enormous. Often times when we consider how much we have to do, how far we want to go, how much we have to learn, and how many children we are trying to reach we let go of the vision. But change is less daunting if we think about the childhood game Mother May I where the designated leader of the game tells each player (all of whom are at a starting line) how many "baby steps" or "giant steps" to take in her direction.

The object of the game is to reach "Mother" first. Mother may say, "Jan, take four baby steps" or "Jan, take two giant steps," and I, after seeking permission, respectfully move where and how she directs. I remember my amazement as a young child when I realized that 11 baby steps could equal one giant step. You can win the game taking nothing but baby steps. This meant that even if Mother was only assigning me baby steps, I still had room to hope. What a triumph!

When I began writing this book, I was overwhelmed by the very idea of it. So I made some decisions. I chose to concentrate on the process of getting my thoughts and experiences nailed to the page rather than on the final product. A writer friend had told me that if I would write just one page a day, I would have a whole book in a year.

So I didn't let myself think about the whole book, or if all these bits and pieces would ever even become a book. I committed to writing a little each day. I chose to use the writing as an exercise in reflection on our work, rather than the pursuit of an end product. I don't think the project would have ever been completed otherwise. It would have been too daunting, and I would have been too discouraged. However, when you think of just one page at a time, in the end you look back and say, "Where did all those pages come from?" We must think about big change this way, seeing only baby steps when we look forward but seeing the inevitable accumulation of miles and miles of giant steps when we look back.

This is how we must approach change in our schools—one baby step at a time. Say, "I'm going to get the bookroom going. That's all I'm going to worry about right now," and then, "I'm going to do a few guided-reading demonstrations," and then, "I'm going to read a book about comprehension instruction." Eventually we will be able to look back and see an accumulation of little accomplishments that add up to big progress and make it easier to move yet another baby step forward.

What Does Change Look Like?

All teaching, whether in a classroom or as a coach, is an act of rehearsal. It is the accumulation of rehearsals that forms the experience and marks our growth, however constant, however gradual, however daunting. This accumulation helps us own the change as we learn that what may seem overwhelming is actually possible. This understanding is more than a collection of lessons and theory. It has heart because it is composed of our individual milestones of progress.

Change around our schools will manifest in at least two areas: instruction and community. Both are part of any school, and whether strong or weak, they are indicators of change. When there is a positive change in instruction, there is literally new movement in that area. The room gets rearranged, the materials get reorganized, and the teaching becomes deliberate, maybe even temporarily clumsy. This collection of small activities helps to create larger shifts across a school.

The second area where a coach might witness change is in the sense of community in a school. Big change in a school community is indicated by many smaller activities, whether helpful or detrimental. Little by little, the community in a school can be dismantled by actions such as gossiping, complaining, or sabotaging. On the other hand, the cumulative building of positive actions, such as demonstrating encouragement or assuming goodwill, can form the foundation of significant, positive change.

Developing Visions of Literacy

Although we build significant change on concentrated but small activities, a coach who is working on isolated strategies with teachers will have a hard time developing any depth of literacy understanding and is unlikely to bring about significant change across his entire school. When I began working as a coach, I knew that I needed to somehow communicate a schoolwide vision of what our classrooms could be and the power that teachers possessed to bring about that change. Eventually this became a path of supported discovery. If we give teachers materials and guide them to look in a particular direction, one day, if we are patient with the process, one of them will eventually say, "Wow!" and this will be the stone that sends ripples across the school.

Although a ripple can begin with an individual simple exclamation, I wanted to communicate to the entire faculty my reflections on our long-term goals. I had a vision that teachers would develop a deep understanding of the reading process, build a common vocabulary around these understandings, and activate these understandings to plan for solid instruction. I wanted them to reach a high level of sophistication in their thinking around literacy. The teachers were all in different places in terms of their instructional experiences and literacy understandings, and I wanted to try to get everyone to a common point so we would have a shared base of understanding.

I was not at all sure how I would facilitate this high level of literacy thinking across the school, much less where to start. Such confusion, however, seems to be the trademark of visionary thinking. If we know exactly how to realize our vision, then it probably isn't lofty enough. Challenge is intrinsic to any authentic vision. Barkley and Bianco (2005) write, "A vision does not double as a goal or an objective; a vision belongs in a larger state" (p. 87).

After much thought about the aforementioned vision, I decided to begin with a whole-school professional learning session to explore the basics of the reading process and initiate a conversation around literacy. I prepared a digital presentation and, wanting to take advantage of this opportunity, I worked hard to make it as interesting, thought provoking, engaging, and comprehensive as I could. I used any tools I could find to illustrate how reading works. My favorite was a book that used a made-up alphabet to simulate learning to read. This gave teachers insight into the reading process by dismantling their automated reading behaviors. "Reading" in such a fundamental way also developed in them a fresh sense of empathy for their students.

The response to the meeting was enthusiastic. The meeting served to launch a vision, however blurry, that our teachers would be literacy "experts" and that this would affect their instruction in positive ways. This early gathering presented teachers with basic information about the reading process, on which I assertively built and extended in the individual teachable moments that arose in hallways, in classrooms, and at lunch tables. Eventually, we had a common place on which to stand.

This commonality of effort toward a public vision gave us energy. We had a place to put our focus. Joyce, Showers, and Rolheiser-Bennett (1987) write,

> As we design and implement more substantial staff development systems, what will sustain us will be the shared vision of schools where the effects of teaching and curricular practices are pyramided to generate learning energy vastly above what has ever existed in this nation or any other. (p. 22)

So a vision is not just a shared idea of the best we imagine a context can be; it is the accumulated force and spirit that are generated when a school universally sees the vision and vigorously pursues it.

A literacy coach can be critical in this pursuit. We can help develop a sense of community and vision; we can empower teachers to explore the learning they know to be priority. Professional development in the school often grows out of the personal projects initiated by teachers. Teachers are often asked to do too many different things by too many people, and they work within a profession that gives them few, if any, opportunities for reflection. But once literacy coaches begin providing these opportunities, it also becomes our job to move among the teachers while listening, sharing, demonstrating, supporting, encouraging, recognizing, and celebrating growth.

The complexity of teaching can be navigated by the maps we develop with teachers and the routes we create to access the change we are endorsing. We become educational cartographers studying the landscape of classrooms and school communities. Teachers often blaze their own trails; sometimes we can be a compass.

More Than the Sum of Our Parts: Developing the Vision in the School Community

I have 11-year-old twins, each bright, energetic, inspiring, and challenging in his own right. If you put them together, they each have an individual spark in addition to their combined flame. As a pair, they are more than the sum of their parts. To work or play with them together is more than twice as difficult or twice as fun.

The same is true for a school community; if we focus only on individual classrooms and don't work to develop the larger school community, we are taking the slow route to deep change. Literacy coaches are wise to consider the whole school culture. Lyons and Pinnell (2001) write,

> A system is an arrangement of things so intimately connected that they form a unified whole. A system is greater than the sum of its parts. The components of a system work together in *synergy*, producing an effect greater than each could accomplish alone. (p. 44)

Lyons and Pinnell suggest asking a few questions to get a sense of the school culture: "What is it like in the school? How do people feel about being in the school? What do the people in the school spend most of their time doing? How do people work with one another here?" (p. 77). The responses to these questions will give a coach a basic sense of a school. Following are few additional questions to consider as you are exploring a school's culture:

- How does the secretary—the person who first represents the school to the public—interact with teachers and with the public?
- Do you often see people smiling?
- Is there a lot of laughter in faculty meetings?

- Are there parents in the school and, if so, what are they doing, and how does the school receive them?
- How do the adults in the lunchroom interact with the children?
- What are the conversations in the teachers' lounge about?
- What is the atmosphere like in the library?
- Does the administrator make him- or herself present? If so, how does that affect the faculty?

In school cultures where someone is taking care of teachers, the teachers are better able to take care of their students. It is both wonderful and dangerous that one person can play such a pivotal role in changing the culture of an entire school. However, it is true. Those literacy coaches who don't believe this probably haven't worked in a school where there is an authoritative and punitive administrator who lacks emotional intelligence. This one person can affect the way everyone in the school feels about their jobs. These feelings can bring about stress that is unavoidably passed on to the children in large and small ways.

One might argue that the administrator is more likely to influence a school culture than a literacy coach because of the leadership prominence and authority inherent in an administrator's role. This is probably accurate; however, literacy coaches have the opportunity to work with the entire faculty. We are able to treat teachers with respect and care and help them realize their goals. We can play a tremendous role in the development of a positive or negative school culture. The effects of a positive school culture seep into the classrooms and make the work of change less stressful for everyone. Consequently, any work we can do that contributes to a positive school culture may affect every classroom and every student.

Knight (2004) writes,

> [A]n instructional coach has to be more than an expert in instructional practices. She or he is part coach and part anthropologist, advising teachers on how to contend with the challenges and opportunities they face while recognizing each school's unique culture. (p. 33)

Attending to the whole school happens directly through our efforts across all classrooms and indirectly through our efforts in individual classrooms.

Resisting Negative Stereotypes

The previous section may imply that change can been easy; I think this is rarely—if ever—true. In my school, as in most, not everyone shared the same beliefs about literacy, their own stage of growth, and the measures we should take to improve. There was a significant amount of discomfort in our building, some animated discussions, and a few dire predictions. However, I have learned that such discussions are healthy symptoms of an authentic change process, and we need to respect them. Change is never easy; if we think it is, we are probably only "pretending" to change—just like I pretended to be a grownup when I dressed up in my mother's high heels. I may have looked like an adult in the mirror, but I didn't yet understand the realities of getting a job, paying bills, or developing wrinkles like crow's feet. Adulthood was just a game for me, just as quick-and-easy change in schools usually is as well.

Are Teachers Really Resistant?

I am often bothered by negative comments about how educators don't like change. More specifically, I have heard literacy coaches and other educational leaders describe teachers as *resistant* to change. I have been troubled by this term for some time now, and my thinking has evolved to consider it inaccurate at best, unfair at worst. In some contexts the word *resistant* is positive. For example, people who bring about political change often resist the status quo, and it is considered admirable to be a part of "the resistance." However, when the term *resistant* is used in educational contexts, it usually involves someone in a leadership position trying to get teachers to do something differently and perceiving them as uncooperative.

The subtext of *resistant* suggests that teachers don't know what is best for them, that coaches and administrators know more than teachers, and that teachers' refusal to change may mean that they are lazy, negative, cowardly, or even dimwitted—which obviously they are not. *Resistant* tends to have negative connotations that, however subtle, push us deeper into the niche of having to *do* something *to* teachers (e.g., persuade, convince, direct, or change). If we take this stance, teachers are understandably going to distrust us. Consequently, real change will be thwarted by the attitudes of the leaders who are trying to facilitate it.

We are wise to adopt a stance of healthy respect and attentiveness to the reluctance that teachers exhibit. If a horse I am riding shies from going into the brush, maybe there is a rattlesnake there. Voices of dissent can be safety nets that warn us of danger and prevent disasters. Their absence should be a cause for concern. Teachers are intelligent and intuitive, and any hesitancy they have toward change is probably with good reason. We should respect teachers' tentativeness, and we should work to explore and resolve the barriers they are experiencing and support them through the confusion and dissonance that is innate to change. Wheatley (2002) writes about the sense of disorientation that is a precursor to progress:

> We can't be creative if we refuse to be confused. Change always starts with confusion; cherished interpretations must dissolve to make way for the new. Of course it's scary to give up what we know, but the abyss is where newness lives. Great ideas and inventions miraculously appear in the space of not knowing. If we can move through the fear and enter the abyss, we are rewarded greatly. (p. 37)

Usually if teachers are not readily pursuing the change we are promoting there is a valid reason, which may or may not be part of the school context. In addition, they are probably wrestling with the anxiety associated with trying something new. If we consider teachers as people before we consider them as educators, we must then acknowledge that they have personal and professional needs beyond our understanding.

If we are unsuccessful in identifying the barrier to change, then we must give the teacher the benefit of the doubt and assume that she has a solid reason for not adopting the recommended change, even if we can't see it. Maybe the problem is *us* and the way we have introduced, shared, addressed, suggested, or pushed the change. Marks and Gersten (1998) write,

> When a change agent feels there is resistance, researchers of professional development should note this as merely evidence of other important contextual issues, and that attempting to understand these issues can be extremely valuable for refining practice, and ultimately, for benefiting students. (p. 55)

If we assume the best of the teacher, we support her in her choice not to change when personal or professional factors are presently inhibiting her.

Anderson (2001) uses a swimming analogy to illustrate how teachers should be supported through change. She writes of her own frustrations as a first-year teacher who lacked the structural support and collaborative environment that could have helped her help her students. She speculates, "What if that struggling first-year teacher had been given 'water wings'—small supports for the unpracticed swimmer, not enough to bear the entire weight of the body, but valuable assistance while you strengthen your technique and your confidence?" (p. 738).

Literacy coaches are the water wings. We are the training wheels. We are whatever that teacher needs us to be, whether tremendous or miniscule, and the difficulty in this is that sometimes neither we nor the teachers know exactly what that is, and educational leaders often interpret such uncertainty as resistance.

Helping the coachee figure out what she needs is part of a literacy coach's job, as is encouraging her, guiding her, cheering her, and comforting her. However, while literacy coaching brings with it many stressors, standing on the sidelines and encouraging someone to take a risk is easier in many ways than taking that risk ourselves.

Perhaps I sound like a "softy;" you may be thinking, at what point do we "lay down the law"? Well, if a teacher is truly a cog in the wheel of reform, we can apply some pressure by continuing to present information and engaging in conversation. However, the question of mandated or grass roots change is one we don't even have to address. If there is law to be laid, literacy coaches are not the ones to lay it. We must leave law laying and personnel issues to the administration, even if the administration is not addressing them.

Diving in to Change

Recently, my son began taking diving lessons. He goes to the pool on a university campus where college and professional swimmers and divers practice and compete. There are six diving boards, each a little higher than the last. Despite the fact that Christopher is extremely excited about diving, he is afraid to jump off the higher boards. He and the other beginning divers all walk out onto the highest board and stare down at the water more than 30 feet below. One by one, they all look at the coach standing beside them, shake their heads, turn around, and walk back down. I certainly don't blame them.

Jumping into a change is like jumping off a high dive; it's scary and once we do it we can't really change our minds. We understandably want to spend a little time looking off the ledge, considering what we are about to do. No one says, "Oh, he's a resistant diver." No one looks down on someone who is resistant to jumping off a high dive. This is an appropriate fear, an evolutionary mechanism, and we appreciate it. We look up at the diving board and encourage teachers to jump, all the while saying to ourselves, "Oh, boy, that's really high. I'm glad I'm not up there."

Lyons and Pinnell (2001) address the discomfort associated with change:

> When people are learning something new, dissonance is not only inevitable but desirable. Dissonance sharpens your thinking and brings comparisons to mind that clarify understanding. We call this "good dissonance," because it serves a useful purpose in learning. Within a trusting context, dissonance works for you. (p. 141)

It is our biological nature to resist dissonance. Why then do we consider it anything other than normal when we see teachers do it? It is often because we are experiencing external pressure to *make* teachers change, to raise test scores, and to lift the level of instruction. When this happens, we pass our pressure on to teachers. If a supervisor or administrator was not banging on our back door, we would be less distracted from trying to take care of the teacher standing on our front porch.

In addition to casting teachers in a negative light, referring to teachers as *resistant* also makes me uncomfortable because it subtly positions the person advocating for the change in a position above the teacher rather than beside her. It discredits teachers' expertise as professionals. This is not to say that there aren't classrooms where significant improvements don't need to be made or that there aren't some issues on which we need to exercise our expertise. However, we should approach teachers as fellow learners, each of us trying to move another baby step forward.

We can use fairer terms than *resistant* to describe the way people sometimes respond to outside forces of change: reluctant, hesitant, reflective, thoughtful, studying, thinking, researching, or cautious. We might say of teachers, "She's still studying the change," or "He's still processing." These statements, of course, imply that the teacher is being given some choice in the matter. While some politicians and administrations may not understand it, the reality is that the teacher *does* have a choice in the matter, and the literacy coach should give him time to process, study, research, think, reflect, and consider so when he does decide to change, it will grow out of his own priorities and understandings and be more likely to last.

At some point, teachers may need us to nudge them because processing change is more comfortable than acting on it, but, as I've discussed, we must give teachers the benefit of the doubt if we want to survive this job. Negativity is an awful contagion, and when it begins spreading, literacy coaches can find themselves in the middle of an epidemic with little idea of how to help anyone get well. Initiating a change by casting teachers in a negative light is not going to make things change any faster. Any change adopted in this context is likely to be superficial and short-lived.

Giving Teachers Credit Where Credit Is Due

Despite often being labeled *resistant*, the reality is that teachers do constantly change. They change their practice, their philosophies, their schedules, their plans for the day's lesson, their seating charts, their management systems, and their interactions with children. I don't think that someone can be an educator, certainly not a strong one, without embracing change, because teaching is all about trial, error, and adaptation.

Teaching involves constantly working through "titrations." For example, if a doctor prescribes someone a new medication, she may conduct a titration, giving the patient a new prescription each week, and slightly increasing the dosage with each prescription. This continues until the perfect dosage for the patient is determined. On a simpler level, if we put sugar in our tea, we conduct a titration. We put in one spoonful, taste, add another spoonful, and taste again, until it satisfies us.

Teachers are continually working through titrations. They teach, they observe, they teach some more. They arrange the furniture in their rooms and then observe to find out which parts of the arrangement work. They explain something one way, assess understanding, then explain it another way. Teachers are constantly measuring the effects of their instruction, tasting that metaphorical glass of tea to make sure that they have done all that is needed in order to secure the greatest benefit for students. Toll (2005) addresses the issue of teacher change:

> Teachers are practical people, and teachers base a lot of their learning on action research, even though they don't always label it as such. They see a

problem in their classroom, they make some changes, and they see if those changes have been effective. (p. 29)

We must support teachers as they exercise their right to be involved in the changes in their work. We have all been part of district "staff development" that decides that such-and-such is what teachers need. However, teachers, more than anyone, if given the opportunity and the community, are more connected to their own growth areas and the needs of students. We can register the resistance to change that comes from our teachers and know that it is there, not because teachers don't care about students and not because they don't acknowledge areas in their instruction that they could improve, but because our system for professional development traditionally leaves them out of the planning and decision-making processes.

Toll's (2005) thoughts on teacher resistance to change are enlightening to me. She tells the story of an educator, Bob, who she perceived as rather set in his ways and resistant to change. One day Bob inquired about some impending district changes and went on to relate that he was good at handling change. Toll was stunned because she did not think of Bob as being receptive to change. A few years later, she thought about Bob differently:

> I thought about Bob with a wider perspective, and here's what occurred to me: At the time of our conversation about middle school, Bob had just seen his only daughter off to college. In addition, he had just dealt with the death of a relative who was living in his home. Bob had a great deal of change going on in his life; it just wasn't easily visible at work. (p. 28)

Perhaps many of those teachers we perceive as resisting change are actually changing in big ways in different contexts. Maybe they need less participation in change at school because things at home are changing dramatically. Maybe a parent is sick or a marriage is shaky. Some will argue that our home lives shouldn't affect our work lives. I would argue that the two are inextricably connected.

Supporting Change

In our work with teachers, we want them to develop autonomy in their instructional decision making and to own the changes that we have helped them claim. This teaching toward independence is a characteristic in many training fields. The following is an analogy of one parallel field that, from beginning to end, mirrors the dynamics of some relationships between teachers and coaches. It addresses motivation to change, reluctance, automaticity, trust, success, and celebration.

Suppose I decide that I need to lose weight and get in shape, and you are a personal trainer that I am considering hiring. I have three children, a demanding day job, and passion for writing that consumes every spare moment. My lifestyle habits are unhealthy and I have known it for some time. However, recent physical indicators such as reduced stamina, tightening waistlines, and general fatigue have pushed me into a discomfort zone that has prompted me to pursue change.

I interview you first to make sure that you know what you are doing. You talk to me about your experience and your philosophy. You knowledgeably inquire about my concerns and needs. You look healthy yourself. There is a banana and a bottle of water on your desk as opposed to the bag of chips and soft drink on mine. So I, with thin but optimistic confidence in your expertise, hire you. "Perhaps," I think to myself, "if I learn that you are unqualified, I will not have to go through with this."

Next, after my confidence has thickened a bit, after I have read about you on the Internet, and talked with a former client, I schedule an appointment for you to assess my present level of fitness. You are going to present me with data, and I am not looking forward to it. This is very risky for me. I'm very vulnerable and feel exposed, literally and metaphorically. I have just enough confidence in you to put myself in your hands, just enough discomfort with the present situation to want to change, and just enough fear to make me look for excuses to change my mind.

I don't change my mind, however, and I show up for my appointment with you. First, you weigh me and compare my weight to what a person my age and height should weigh. You determine my ratio of body fat to muscle and again tell me what research indicates is an appropriate ratio for me. I am, of course, now thinking with certainty that this was not a good idea. I would leave, but I am invested in you financially and emotionally, and I really do want to be a better steward of my health.

Then, to add insult to injury, you take photographs of me from all sides to serve as my "before" shots. I engage in a fair amount of self-deprecating humor in an effort to protect myself from what I imagine you are already thinking. You recognize my feelings of failure; however, knowing that acknowledging my present condition will facilitate my commitment to the work ahead, you don't gloss over these feelings or discourage me from having them.

Nonetheless, you are sensitive to my needs. You don't criticize me. You don't pass judgment. You remain objective, even kind, and just present me with research-based facts. You ask me to do some simple exercises to assess my current strength, and I hesitantly oblige, despite a desperate wish not to know any more about how well I'm not doing. My inability to perform the exercises without becoming quickly fatigued contributes to my commitment to change.

You know that I have enough to think about and struggle through. You are sensitive to the fact that too much discomfort will overwhelm me, and I will feel that the task is just too big to tackle. You remind me that you know how to help me and that you are confident, because you have worked with many people, that I can be successful. You give me a written summary of the data you have collected; I schedule our next appointment, and go home tired, overwhelmed, and a little bit hopeful.

I knew that my clothes had gotten a little tight and that there were certain things I wouldn't even wear anymore. I knew that I avoided clothes shopping because I thought I had gone up another size. I knew that I was more tired at the end of the day and that I was less likely to walk when I could ride. I knew that I wasn't eating healthily or drinking enough water. However, all these general understandings become realities when you show me data. The actual numbers bring everything into focus because they are not subjective, and they are, as is often the case, worse than I had imagined.

Later at home, I reconcile myself with my responsibility in the situation. I didn't know it was this bad. I actually work through a process similar to a grieving process over the next few hours, moving from anger to denial and all the way through to acceptance. In the end, I rally around the fact that I can do something about the problem and that you are going to help me.

At our next session, I am ready to follow your instructions to the letter. I am hungry for any information you want to give me. I ask questions. I take notes. I want to do exactly what you say down to the last detail: repetitions, weight, and frequency. I listen carefully; you reassure me. You demonstrate; we practice together. I try the exercises myself, and you coach me until I am doing them properly.

You give me just enough information to get me moving forward but not so much that I am overwhelmed. You limit the amount of weight I bear in the exercises so that I can practice and habituate my form. You watch over me to make sure I learn these procedures well and accurately in the beginning so that I will be successful in the end and avoid frustration in the process. You are positive; I am hopeful.

In a few days, I return. You encourage me some more. You watch me and you tell me what I am doing well. You clarify my misconceptions. Because you have planned for my success, the routine is enjoyable even though it is hard. You guide me to work hard enough to know I am accomplishing something but not so hard that I want to quit. I begin to visit the gym regularly and enjoy the psychological benefits of accumulated success. You make a point to see me when I am there, and you continue to support me. You point out slight variations that will make my workout more effective. I go to you as I have questions.

You have intentionally started me at a level at which I will progress quickly. You have set me up for early success. Then, you begin to encourage me in other areas. You recommend some vitamin supplements. You tell me where I can buy the freshest vegetables. You engage me in a conversation about how I feel about the work and ask if there is anything else you can do.

After a couple of weeks of consistent work, you bring me a journal to keep a record of my experience. I begin to reflect on the process. I am beginning to see some progress. I am able to correctly perform all the exercises you have given me. Every time I feel my commitment begin to flag, you are at my elbow giving me the support I need. I begin to tune in to my own progress, to recognize my needs, and to articulate my strengths and weaknesses. I have moved into independence in some areas, and you are showing me some new things while continuing to support me in others. Occasionally I have the opportunity to help someone who is new to the gym. I offer them encouragement, answer questions about the equipment, and demonstrate correct form.

Then after a period of time that is long enough to demonstrate progress, but not so long that I have grown weary or hit a plateau, you show me new data. We work through the same steps we worked through in our first data-gathering session. Inevitably, the numbers are better, perhaps dramatically. They have to be, because you have given me research-based strategies to use, made sure that I understood them, and supported me as I grew to own them. You are confident in my success because you have knowledgeably guided and supported me, and this confidence communicates your respect for me.

You know that this next presentation of data is critical. These data need to be worth celebrating and, because you have thoughtfully attended to my work and I have made a sincere effort, they are. This success carries me to another, and another, and another. It becomes an upward spiral that grew out of a very strategic, systematic approach to supporting and motivating me. In the process, I have grown to trust you. We have developed a relationship that allows us to safely be honest with each other, and we have developed a deep emotional connection.

This analogy matches very closely what literacy coaches can do—we coach teachers as the teachers take their own visions for growth and change and nurture them into reality by taking one step at a time. We assume that teachers want to teach their students well, and we help them look closely at their practices. We don't just dump data in their laps, however, and leave them. We encourage them, we tell them we know ways that they can teach more of their children to read successfully, and we promise that we will be with them as they work through it all. Then we keep our promises, and teachers are successful. Then they move on to support other teachers working to change.

Souvenirs

The attention educational authors and researchers give to the topic of change is directly related to the difficulty it represents and its significance in our work; all are mountainous. The enormity and slowness of change can be daunting. The challenge of literacy coaching through the exercise of change is in helping others to see it in manageable pieces when looking forward and as an accumulated whole when looking back. In the midst of all this change, we must resist labeling teachers as resistant and must instead respect their healthy inclination to make sure there is water in the pool before they dive.

The Work:
Stretching Ourselves

CHAPTER 6

Teaching Toward Independence: Teachers as Professional Learners

"They know enough who know how to learn."
Henry Adams, *The Education of Henry Adams*, 1999, p. 256

I have a new camera. It is a digital camera that is much smarter than I. My husband has been a professional photographer for years, and his expertise far surpasses mine. When I take pictures with my new camera, I'm inclined to let it do the thinking for me. My husband, however, is constantly teaching me and pushing me to explore the deep understandings that support photography and the more complex workings of my camera. Setting the camera on automatic and pointing in the direction of something may give me instant gratification, but it is also likely to reduce my need to think. This doesn't do much for my skill level. On the other hand, if I take the time to study apertures, shutter speeds, lenses, and light, I have the theory with which to knowledgeably manipulate my practice.

One of the most important roles for coaches is that of respecting teachers as professionals. This is demonstrated as we support teachers in developing comprehensive understandings of the complexities of the reading process. These maps of understanding will support them as they navigate their instructional courses with children. Deep understandings influence both the long-range planning inherent to capitalizing on the cumulative nature of literacy learning and the moment-to-moment decisions that have the potential to draw a connected path of learning.

In isolation, knowing a particular literacy program does not develop such skill in teachers. Commercial programs can deprofessionalize educators, setting their decision making and responses on automatic. Individual programs will not teach teachers to think broadly and deeply about reading or its supporting processes unless the programs are complemented by professional learning that develops teachers' expertise in understanding why a particular program is suggesting a particular action. For example, if a program uses Elkonin (1973) boxes, commonly referred to as sound boxes, to teach phonemic awareness, a teacher can follow the directions in a published program and be successful at using Elkonin boxes. However, if a teacher understands the purpose for using Elkonin boxes and the hierarchy of phonemic awareness skills that children generally acquire, then she can modify this strategy to individualize the choices she makes for her students.

Often literacy coaches are charged with implementing a new reading program. Many are even hired for this specific purpose. The related professional learning that the literacy coach plans often evolves around supporting the teachers as they learn the teacher's guide and become familiar with the ancillary materials. However, if a literacy coach is not strategic, this can be limiting for a school. Commercial programs can serve as a scaffold for the growth of teachers, but literacy coaches must be vigilant in helping teachers avoid long-term dependence on purchased programs.

If we must use a commercial program as our core focus, we should exercise great care not to let the program dictate our instructional philosophies. Unfortunately, we often have little say about the programs our schools and districts choose for us to support in classrooms. We can, however, know the strengths and shortcomings of the programs and the theory behind them. In addition, we can encourage teachers to look intelligently and critically at the programs they are given to use. Teaching teachers how to critically examine literacy materials against their growing reading expertise gives them a strategy they can continue to use to promote their own learning, independent of you.

If teachers have a well-developed knowledge base around literacy theory and research, then they will be able to evaluate what a program is telling them to do. They will say, "This makes sense because..." or, "This is not instructionally sound because we know that beginning readers...." Commercial programs seek mass appeal, and therefore, utilize a broad approach, trying to be all things to all teachers (or to whomever is making the literacy decisions). Thus, their content often oscillates with the politics of reading and pays homage to the latest trends. Killion (2003) writes,

> As the No Child Left Behind Act increases funding for professional development in literacy, a critical question becomes whether we produce teachers who can implement a program as it is designed or teachers who understand literacy processes and can select appropriate instruction based on their understanding of their students. This dichotomy is the crux of the debate in developing appropriate professional development programs for teachers of literacy. (p. 10)

If teachers have a background in literacy and deep understandings about how children learn to read and write, a collection of resources they have judged to be excellent according to their knowledge of literacy, and the freedom to be decision makers, they will probably be thoughtful consumers of commercial products and be able to tailor their instruction to the specific needs of their students.

Programmatic teaching has been a focus due to legislation in the United States such as Reading First, a subpart of Title 1 of the No Child Left Behind Act of 2001 (2002). In most cases, teachers were given little choice about the programs their schools and districts adopted. Literacy coaches were hired and a big part of their jobs became supporting teachers as they implemented the programs. In such a context, a coach must advocate for the opportunities to facilitate deep literacy learning with teachers as it parallels the content of the program. This is not easy, and the school or district leadership may apply pressure to bring about change quickly.

However, no school claims an abundance of time when addressing literacy reform. The days spent deliberating over programs and materials are often considered days lost for children who are already behind. But time pressures do not validate eliminating the step of providing teachers solid foundations in literacy understandings.

This is yet another lesson I have learned the hard way. If we rush professional inquiry and study, we are likely to end up farther behind than we were when we began. The trick is to let the urgency of the instructional situation push us to focus even more intensely on the knowledge base teachers need to make wise decisions within the district-established, programmatic parameters.

If we become the facilitators of the adopted reading series, regardless of the quality of the series, rather than facilitators of teacher learning about the reading process and literacy instruction, we will limit ourselves, our teachers, and the long-term progress of our schools. Teachers may not have enough information to filter out the inappropriate tasks suggested by the teacher's guides and, when reading texts are up for adoption again and the district program changes, we will have to start over.

Commercial programs do give school districts the consistency that they desperately want—that is, every child in the district receives similar instruction. However, this consistency is merely an illusion. A district superintendent could be tempted by the quick fix of a mandated program to achieve consistency; however, consistency of understandings that support sound instruction is a more authentic and rewarding goal.

Again, I have learned through my experiences and, while they were valuable for me, I would like to spare other coaches the frustration. The level of consistency where all classrooms look exactly the same is unattainable and unnecessary. Literacy coaches can maximize the value of the commercial programs their school districts adopt by exploring the literacy theory behind the lessons the teacher's manuals suggest. Literacy coaches can then share these understandings with teachers so that they and the teachers will be able to use these resources wisely.

Where to Begin: Helping Teachers Set Priorities for Their Learning

As in any learning context, teachers bring with them a variety of background experiences and varying levels of reading expertise. In one professional learning situation we may be working with a first-year teacher and a teacher with 10 years of experience in Reading Recovery. The variety in these skill and experience levels dictates that most of the groundwork with teachers is laid in group settings while the work specific to teacher needs is often addressed in individual conversations with teachers and in time spent in their classrooms.

The work of literacy coaches in classrooms must attend to four areas of instruction and professional growth: (1) management of materials, time, and students; (2) reading theory and pedagogy; (3) instructional competence; and (4) reflection. These areas define the general hierarchy of understanding and competence we need to support in classrooms. For example, if a coach goes into a classroom and watches a teacher efficiently navigate the various managerial tasks of a classroom, then the coach can work primarily on developing the teacher's theory and explore how to apply it practically.

This does not mean that literacy coaches will always work with teachers in these areas in isolation. Developing classroom skill is not linear, and educational absolutes are few. Please do not let this list of coaching priorities deter you from making the decisions that are best for the teachers in your school. Generally, however, there are four areas that may need our coaching attention. Figure 2 illustrates the relationship between these areas. Note that these areas parallel the characteristics of an effective literacy coach (Figure 1, page 35).

Management of Materials, Time, and Students

A wealth of theory and content knowledge will have no value if a teacher doesn't support it by effectively managing materials, schedules, and children. Sometimes it feels as if working with a teacher on managing a pencil-sharpening routine is far removed from literacy instruction. It would be easy and logical for us to say, "That's not my job." However, these seemingly small managerial issues can completely derail instruction and encroach on the boundaries of a literacy lesson from all sides.

Frey and Kelly (2002) studied the effects of staff development, modeling, and coaching on the teacher implementation of interactive writing. They found that

> a significant pattern emerged in the types of concerns teachers held. It seemed that by coaching teachers as they worked through the more mundane elements at the procedural level, such as class management, they were able to break through to student-centered instruction over time. (p. 183)

When a coach helps a teacher negotiate management challenges, the interaction produces tremendous payoffs and makes the work of fine-tuning instruction possible. Furthermore, the domain of management is a safe place to begin a literacy coaching relationship. In this area, it is easy

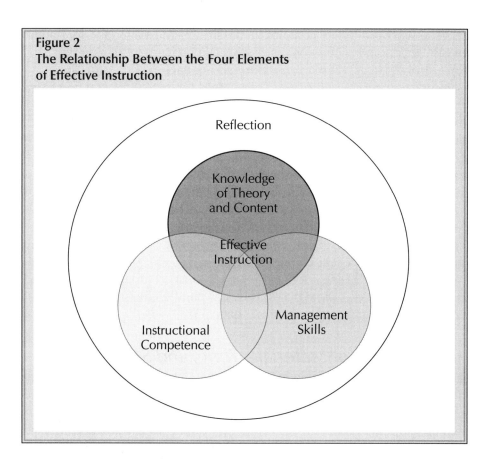

Figure 2
The Relationship Between the Four Elements of Effective Instruction

to be objective, there tends to be less emotional investment, and improvement is obvious.

Reading Theory and Pedagogy

The next major area for professional learning involves studying and exploring reading theory and the strategies it supports. I am speaking primarily of one-on-one theory work rather than the work of building knowledge through group professional learning sessions. One might argue that literacy coaches could skip reading theory and go straight to instructional strategies. However, if we do so, we are likely to find teachers less prepared to adapt to the individual needs of children and less likely to take instructional risks.

Instructional Competence

The third area of professional learning involves the combination of the previous two areas. Theory and strategy knowledge in isolation will offer little toward teaching a child to read, and we have all met teachers who have sophisticated understandings of literacy but are unable to translate those into effective classroom practice. Similarly, a smoothly managed classroom can be peppered with failing students. These areas must move from the cognitive to the practical realm. Teachers must use these theories, strategies, and management systems and integrate them in order for their knowledge to become expertise.

Reflection

As teachers accumulate knowledge and instructional strategies, literacy coaches need to support them in their work of reflection. Reflectiveness is a prerequisite in the effectiveness of teachers. Reflectiveness involves the analysis of the parts against the big picture, reconstruction when instruction does not go well, and giving in to the healthy stress that keeps us moving forward. There is no growth in instructional skill without reflection; it is a strategy that teachers can use in any context and creates a system of learning that supports itself.

Phases of Learning

In addition to exploring target areas for growth, coaches need to consider where a teacher is along a learning continuum relative to each targeted area. Given the vast amount of information teachers need to assimilate, coaches will continually make decisions about whether to introduce something new or to support the further refinement of a previously explored concept or strategy. In doing so, it is helpful to consider the five levels of understanding that teachers may reach. Within each level, I have integrated elements that facilitate a gradual release of responsibility (Pearson & Gallagher, 1983) from the coach to the teacher. These phases are described in Table 2 and illustrated in Figure 3.

The Initiating Phase

This phase represents a teacher's early introductions to the concept or skill. The hallmark of this phase is questioning. Professional learning

Table 2
Comparison of Phases of Learning

Phase	Hallmark Behavior/ Emotion	Coaching Role	Professional Learning/ Gradual Release	Challenges
Initiating	Questioning	Coaching toward understanding	May simplify complicated procedures and concepts into basic components; coach does the "heavy lifting"	Avoiding confusion
Clarifying	Fear and/ or anxiety	Coaching toward confidence	Clarifying misunderstandings; demonstrating, collaborating, observing; some responsibility shifted to teacher	Noticing misunderstandings before they are habituated
Cultivating	Repetition	Coaching toward automaticity	Solidifying understandings; coach and teacher share responsibility equally	Might need to return to Clarifying Phase to address additional misunderstandings
Culminating	Celebration	Coaching toward ownership	Fine-tuning and facilitating celebration; teacher does the "heavy lifting"	Must decide to explore something new or take present practice to the next phase
Inventing	Sophisticated thought	Coaching toward flexibility	Often one one one; manipulates and adapts practice in original ways; teacher has all of the responsibility	Time spent experimenting limits time spent initiating

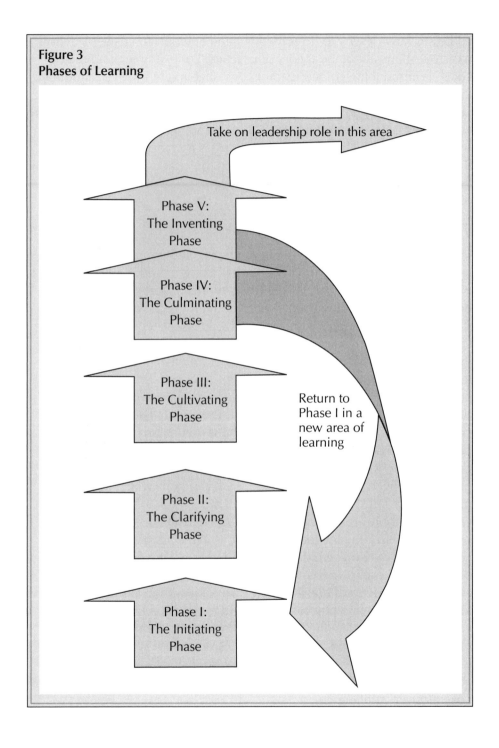

Figure 3
Phases of Learning

Take on leadership role in this area

Phase V:
The Inventing
Phase

Phase IV:
The Culminating
Phase

Phase III:
The Cultivating
Phase

Return to
Phase I in a
new area of
learning

Phase II:
The Clarifying
Phase

Phase I:
The Initiating
Phase

addresses how or why to do something and attempts to answer teachers' basic questions about the theory or practice. For example, if a literacy coach is introducing guided reading, this stage might involve introducing the basic steps, such as book introduction, student reading, and teaching point. At this point in learning, literacy coaches may need to oversimplify content decisions that require deep understandings. They can do this by breaking these decisions into explicit steps as a scaffold for teachers. Responsibility for the work rests mostly on the coach at this point. During this phase, we *coach toward understanding*.

The Clarifying Phase

In this phase, the teacher is just beginning to attempt application of the learning. He is probably not much further along in understanding than he was in the previous phase. The hallmark of this phase is anxiety, fear, or both. Teachers who have been excited about implementing a new strategy find that actually doing so involves a risk. Literacy coaches have to scaffold and encourage teachers heavily during this phase. If we are

thorough in clarifying misunderstandings during this phase, we will set teachers up for success in the next phase. Responsibility for the work begins to shift to the teacher, but the coach still carries most of the weight of the work and provides steady support. Professional learning at this point addresses specific misunderstandings, particularly those that are presenting as patterns across the school, and works to solidify any procedures or skills. For example, in professional learning regarding guided reading, a coach might revisit the basic steps while addressing misunderstandings, such as spending too much time introducing the text, engaging in round-robin reading, or overly focusing on a particular cueing system during the teaching point. In the classroom, a literacy coach's work may involve demonstrating for, collaborating with, or observing the teacher, depending on the level of understanding he exhibits. It is wise for literacy coaches working with teachers in this phase to demonstrate before observing, because the effort is likely to save a coach time and the teacher discomfort. Inevitably, there have been misunderstandings, and demonstrating clarifies those without setting the teacher up for failure. For the most part, responsibility for the work is equally shared between the coach and the teacher. During this phase, we *coach toward confidence*.

The Cultivating Phase

In this phase, the teacher begins to really grasp the instructional theory or practice. The hallmark of this phase is repetition. Professional learning will most likely reinforce previously learned ideas with the intent to solidify them. In this phase, literacy coaches direct professional learning about guided reading toward helping the teacher become seamless in her practices and shift her mental energy to adapting to the children's needs. Ideally, a literacy coach has resolved misunderstandings in the clarifying phase, so behaviors practiced by teachers are sound and appropriate. If not, the coach will have to return to the clarifying phase with the teacher, which is likely to be frustrating and discouraging for both. The literacy coach is still decreasingly involved with the work, and responsibility is steadily shifting to the teacher. During this phase, we *coach toward automaticity*.

The Culminating Phase

During this phase, the teacher's hard work is actualized in the habituation of the learned practice and the progress of the students. The hallmark behavior at this phase is celebration. The teacher consistently demonstrates competence in the application. Skills that were intentional in the earlier phases are now automatic, freeing the teacher's attention for fine-tuning. The basics and a little beyond have grown strong out of the extensive root system established in the three preceding phases. Professional learning at this point becomes a matter of fine-tuning practice, sustaining momentum, and facilitating celebration. Observations and conversations with teachers remain important but will be less frequent in regard to this particular practice. Although the coach may provide occasional support, responsibility for the work rests on the teacher. During this phase, we *coach toward ownership*.

Once teachers have negotiated the culminating phase, the coach and the teacher need to decide whether to return to the initiating phase and explore a new theory or practice or to take the present practice to the next level.

The Inventing Phase

In this phase, teachers have the opportunity to mold their practice into new shapes that meet their specific needs. The hallmark of this phase is sophistication of thought. This phase requires a significant amount of problem solving, and a teacher's skill in higher order thinking will be a factor in her success. Coaching at this point is a matter of conferencing with teachers to work through ideas or to think about instruction in a different way. Professional learning at this phase is often one on one and may address sophisticated prompting, alternative grouping strategies, or connecting guided reading to other components of the literacy framework. At this level, teachers feel strong enough in the practice to manipulate and experiment with it. Although the coach may be involved in teacher-initiated collaborative study or planning, the teacher carries full responsibility for the work specific to implementing the strategy. At this point, a teacher may assume a leadership role in this area, facilitating professional learning on the topic and supporting peers. During this phase, we *coach toward flexibility*.

Working with teachers who are able to experiment with and extend their practice is extremely gratifying; however, not all teachers will work at this level in all aspects of literacy instruction. In fact, the complexity of this phase is more demanding than we may realize. There tends to be difficulty in taking the demonstrated skill and successfully accessing it in the classroom. Joyce and Showers (2002) speak to the problem of transfer:

> Both trainers and teachers tend to underestimate the cognitive aspects of implementation—teachers have assumed they have only to see something to use it skillfully and appropriately, and trainers have devoted little or no time during training to attacking the transfer problem. (p. 80)

It is normal, even healthy, for teachers to set up residence in the developing and culminating stages in some areas of their instruction. It may take a teacher up to 25 lessons with a new strategy before he is even ready to expand on it (Showers, Joyce, & Bennett, 1987). At this point, the coaching work becomes a matter of making sure implementation is thorough, authentic, and true to the priorities and vision of the school.

A school will make more progress in literacy growth if the teachers are in the developing and cultivating phases with guided reading, writer's workshop, and word work than if they are at the inventing phase in only one of these areas. Time is the issue here, and coaches and teachers have to make thoughtful decisions. "No one component of the framework is the key to literacy learning; its effectiveness lies in the range of learning contexts that are included" (Lyons & Pinnell, 2001, p. 35).

Creating the Space to Be Different

Teacher needs, personalities, and instructional styles are different, and teachers will be working within different learning phases. In this and other areas, literacy coaches must appreciate the variation across a school. As literacy coaches, we must give teachers some space for instructional individuality. We do not need to be about the business of creating classrooms where every teacher is doing the same thing in the same way at the same time.

There are certain instructional elements that may be the core of our school's literacy growth, but if we do not give teachers room for individuality, we take away some of their valuable energy. Teachers need room to breathe. We give them breathing room by making sure they thoroughly understand why certain things must be done in certain ways and then letting the periphery work take shape as a teacher needs it to. Coaches should be available to help a teacher look at her instruction from a different perspective if necessary, but the teacher should own the general profile of her instruction.

For example, early in my work as a literacy coach, I felt pressure to have a specific literacy "block"—a specific block of time with designated periods for writing, independent reading, read-aloud, guided reading, and so forth. The few literacy coaches I knew at the time were using this and similar models in their schools. This detailed schedule enabled them to make very informed statements about their schools like, "We spend 30 minutes a day reading aloud," or "Teachers teach guided reading right before writer's workshop."

This was appealing to me because these coaches were able to speak knowledgeably about what was going on in their buildings, but because I couldn't nail things down as clearly, I felt I wasn't doing my job as well. On some level, I was indicting my work because I didn't have such specific, standardized information to share about our school.

While other coaches had consistency across classrooms, I had to keep a copy of each teacher's classroom schedule and review it regularly to have any real sense of how their time was allotted. Visiting classrooms was more complicated because schedules were unpredictable across the various classrooms. Scheduling visitors or consultants was difficult because it *seemed* that no one did any particular literacy component at a logical time.

In the end, however, I was glad we made the effort. Supporting the diversity in classroom instruction in our school was less an intellectual decision and more a case of me just not quite knowing how to go about getting everyone on the same page. Since then, however, there have been opportunities to standardize schedules and amounts of time spent on various elements of our literacy work. We have stuck to supporting teachers in maintaining individuality across classrooms within certain parameters. Everyone teaches the various elements of our literacy framework with consistency and regularity. However, if one person likes to sandwich read-aloud between guided reading and writer's workshop, while another likes to start the day with read-aloud, I appreciate these differences for the texture they lend to our instructional day and for the comfort and energy they afford teachers.

Keeping It Simple

There is little that is simple about literacy coaching. Understanding the theory and pedagogy of reading, understanding the personalities and needs of teachers, and understanding the complex intermingling of the two is remarkably complicated. Pinnell and Lyons (1998) address the complex nature of literacy instruction. They write,

> Considering the level of skills needed to teach only one component of the curriculum—guided reading, we argue that teacher education is a complex process, one that can not be accomplished in a few courses or even a few years. (p. 22)

Sometimes I feel as though I am living the weight of this statement. We dedicate enormous amounts of time to guided reading or writer's workshop, and there are so many other things we need to initiate and support until they are solid. Furthermore, we want to build these practices on a strong theoretical base. However, Knight (2004) suggests that literacy coaches should "[m]ake it as easy as possible. If an intervention works and is easy to implement, our experience suggests teachers will use it" (p. 34).

I have learned that teaching to deep understandings doesn't make the work inherently complicated—I do. I can complicate the simplest of tasks. Part of it is, I think, because I have studied a lot about literacy instruction. The other part, I'm sure, has to do with the analytical nature of my brain and my idiosyncratic thought processes. The more a literacy coach studies, the more he knows, and the more he has to make choices about what information to pass along to teachers. Sometimes less information equals deeper understandings and more instruction. Teachers can have a healthy base of literacy knowledge without getting into all the detail a literacy coach might need to explore. This is particularly true when we are trying to make decisions for professional learning sessions. We should not try to tell teachers everything we know all at once, and we don't have to reorganize all our expertise around each decision we make.

Coaches are resident experts on literacy; it is our job to know as much as we can about this one subject so that we can, with the other literacy experts in our schools, make informed decisions about literacy and discern priorities for instruction. However, sifting through the logjam of ideas and information in our heads can dramatically decrease our efficiency. From a classroom perspective and a literacy coaching perspective, having too many choices can make instruction more complicated and possibly even less effective. This does not mean that we just tell teachers what to do. It means that we are selective in the strategies we share, that we always support these strategies with the literacy understandings behind them, and that we continually expand teachers' options by sharing new strategies and new theory at a rate that builds momentum but does not overwhelm them.

Recently we had a Family Literacy Night at our school, and parents came and participated in a writing workshop. It was a clever idea, but I just couldn't get my head around it. I labored over it through the course of a week. Every time I thought about it, my head swam with ideas. I wanted the parents to have several examples to look at so their written pieces wouldn't look like mine. I had an entire book, *Authors in the Classroom: A Transformative Education Process* (Ada & Campoy, 2004), about involving families in writing together. I considered doing a minilesson about choosing a topic, writing with voice, getting pictures in your head, and on and on.... I was overwhelmed and, consequently, I was unable to make a decision.

Daphne Hall, my friend who is an instructional coach and who first conceived of the idea of writing with parents for our literacy night, was at our school one day as the literacy night was drawing close. I explained, probably in the most complicated fashion imaginable, my struggle. She said something like, "You're making things too complicated, *again*." Then she said, "We won't give them an example at all. The minilesson will be about choosing a family story about which to write. We'll have them decide on three family stories, and then we'll have them choose the one that means the most to them. We'll let a few of them share their topics, and then we'll give them blank books and they'll write."

Just like that, Daphne made all the critical decisions associated with the evening while I was still deciding whether we should use markers or colored pencils. Daphne cut through the clutter and made everything simple. It is not that she doesn't have extensive expertise; she does. It is that she was able to efficiently sift and sort that expertise as it related to the context of our Family Literacy Night. She was able to prioritize the decisions that needed to be made so that her energy was directed toward those that mattered most. Daphne was absolutely right, and the writing workshop was a tremendous success by all accounts.

I am slowly learning that, nine times out of 10, simple is better. Furthermore, if I'm working too hard at something, I'm probably making it more complicated than it needs to be. For me, being stuck is often a symptom of overthinking. In the end, all I needed was to give parents and children a positive experience writing together; fortunately, Daphne was there to help me see how to make that happen.

Helping Teachers Keep Things Simple

When teachers make things complicated, it is sometimes a symptom of an illness we don't really mind our teachers catching. It's the I-Understand-Reading-Too-Well Syndrome. As teachers grow in their understandings of the reading process and their skill in supporting children, they will, because they want to help children become better readers, move in the direction of individual instruction. This can actually compromise instruction.

For example, one teacher with whom I work has developed deep understandings around literacy development. She now knows a lot about recognizing particular challenges facing her students and how best to provide support. Almost every term, she comes to me with her children grouped into small, focused groups. This means, of course, that she has too many groups during guided reading. It is marvelous that she understands literacy so deeply and that she is interested in focusing intently on individual needs. However, if she does not have enough time to teach each group, her wonderful intentions may actually impede the progress of her readers.

When teachers truly learn how to teach children to read, they step into the uncomfortable place where most literacy coaches already live. Balancing literacy expertise between the demands of the group and the demands of individuals is the classic reading specialist conundrum. We are forced to strike a balance between helping too much and helping too little, even when we know enough to help everyone if we just had the time. If we try to individualize instruction completely, we will be just as ineffective as we would be if we tried to teach everyone out of the same book. I'm not suggesting that teachers ignore the individual needs of their students but that they judiciously weigh the needs of individuals against the needs of the whole group. So while, unlike Reading Recovery teachers, we do not have the luxury of working with a single child for 30 minutes each day, we do want our teachers' understandings of literacy instruction to be as deep and as strong as those of Reading Recovery teachers, and this mismatch can be stressful for teachers and literacy coaches.

Appreciating Approximations

Acquiring the understandings and skills described throughout this chapter takes time, and we must give teachers opportunities to aim and miss the target—perhaps they will get a little closer to the bull's eye with each attempt. Showers (1985) writes, "We understand and argue for children's needs to acquire component skills of complex behaviors and, through practice, successive approximations of expert performance. Thus, we applaud their efforts in first recitals, junior sports, primitive essays, and early attempts at cooking" (p. 46). Such approximations are necessary exercises for anyone, adult or child, trying to understand and habituate a new skill. Similarly, we have to give teachers room and time to safely and gradually align their approximations with mature implementations of a practice.

This is at once exciting and uncomfortable. We have to protect teachers from themselves. Teachers can't teach five guided reading groups each day without compromising something else or experiencing burnout. So it seems that we are in the precarious position of guiding teachers in the direction of reading understandings that give them the skills to individualize their instruction expertly and then guiding them in the other direction toward meeting the needs within the context of a whole group. This is difficult for teachers and for literacy coaches. Once again, we are faced with an issue of balance.

Souvenirs

We facilitate professional learning for teachers with the goal of expanding their understandings and skill in ways that will manifest in their classrooms. In making related decisions, we must consider the content needs and the levels of understanding that teachers exhibit individually and as a collective. Our purposes must move beyond distributing programmatic information and must hold a hard focus on learning and perpetuating intelligent and effective literacy instruction. We need to share with teachers the mysteries and practicalities of their instructional cameras so that they can use their expertise to assemble sound compositions, own the pictures they take, and recognize themselves as artists.

CHAPTER 7

Developing Trust: The Language of Classroom Visitation

"[T]he difference between the almost right word and the right word is really a large matter—'tis the difference between the lightning bug and the lightning."
Mark Twain, "The Art of Composition," as cited in Neider, C. (Ed.). *Life as I Find It: A Treasury of Mark Twain Rarities*, 2000, p. 228

One night my husband and I were coaching our son, who was almost 2 years old at the time, to pick up his toys and put them back into their basket. We had experienced an epiphany that it was time for him to learn about cleaning up. It was one of these parental "Ahas!" that gives parents momentary panic, causing us to say to ourselves, Oh my goodness! He is going to grow up a slob because he is almost 2 and we have never taught him anything about cleaning up. All the other 2-year-olds have been picking up their own toys for months. Is he developmentally delayed?

So we coached him as he picked up his blocks. We observed his use of strategies. We asked him how he felt about his work. We watched as he became engaged in the task. And when he was finished, we celebrated. I thought about our older twins and how my expectations for them are different. I expect them to put things away properly and to pay attention to the details of their efforts. I rarely celebrate their work without condition. I will say, "Pretty good, Christopher. There's a sock under your bed you missed."

Whenever I spend any time in the classroom of an exceptional teacher, I know that the magic is not in what I see, but in what I know happened in the days, weeks, and months preceding my visit. I believe the cornerstone of any classroom of engaged learners is a sense of connectedness to the teacher and to each other. In some classrooms there even seems to be a familial feeling between the teacher and the students, as if they really have a family bond.

Whenever I watch the dynamics of an incredible classroom community, I inevitably find myself watching a teacher who is focused on the positive in her students, who treats them respectfully, who proffers articulate declarations of their capability, who has made the classroom emotionally rich, and who, consequently, has helped the children invest heavily in their work and develop confidence and independence. The children in these classrooms know they can do amazing things. Such teachers help to persuade each student of his or her intrinsic worth, intelligence, responsibleness, and value.

Are the dynamics of learning significantly different for adults? How does building a school community compare to building a classroom community? Is such positive, supportive interaction transferable to a mature learning context? These questions are worth exploring.

Appreciating Positive Experiences in the Classroom

I experienced a tremendous paradigm shift when I spent a week in a professional learning session with 17 other coaches. Peg Gwyther, our facilitator, gave us a surprisingly simple way to analyze our work. She told us to ask if the experience in question was positive for the learner. For example, was the read-aloud a positive experience for the children? If so, it probably had many elements of a sound read-aloud. Was the postobservation conference a positive experience for the teacher? If so, the coach probably successfully supported him. This doesn't necessarily mean that the read-aloud or the postobservation conference were perfect;

it just means that there was room for celebration and opportunity for a productive conversation about the work.

What a radical way to think! As I considered this, I decided that with only a few basic ideas in place, positive experiences are at the heart of much of our work. If the children didn't have a positive experience during guided reading, there is probably a reason that is tied to instructional delivery and connected to the very basic tenets of reading pedagogy. Was the book too difficult? Was there too much instruction and not enough reading practice? Was the lesson organized well enough to keep downtime from lessening its effect?

If the children had a positive experience, a coach can remind the teacher to celebrate. If not, what are the building blocks of positive experiences that are already in place, and how can a literacy coach thoughtfully help a teacher build on those? Even if the lesson was instructionally unsound, if the children had a positive experience, a literacy coach has a starting point with the teacher, who has a starting point with the children because the experience was positive. How do we maintain the level of joy experienced by the participants and raise the level of instruction?

This goal is also applicable to our work with teachers. Many will say that our work is proven successful or unsuccessful by test scores. There is certainly some truth in this, and I have yet to meet a literacy coach who doesn't analyze test scores to support instructional decision making. But in the immediacy of one lesson and one conference with a teacher, the joy in the experience is a valid measure. If a visit to a classroom is positive, and if we are able to make one suggestion nestled in the safety of noticed strengths, we are much more likely to affect classroom instruction than if we are focused heavily on what is wrong with the instruction. Or even better, we need to support teachers as they learn to identify what they see as the strengths of their instruction and then to plan action that builds on these strengths.

If our experiences in classrooms are not positive, not only are we less likely to affect instruction but we have also compromised our future interactions with the teacher. Was the conference a positive experience for the teacher? This is a question that will define our work as successful or unsuccessful. Again, with a few givens in place, the answer to this question is the answer to many. Why didn't he or she have a positive experience? Did she feel threatened? Did I position myself in a power role? Did I talk too much? Did I give too many suggestions? Did my positive feedback seem hollow or insincere? *Was* my positive feedback hollow or insincere? Did I take over rather than follow her lead? Did I skip the modeling and leave the teacher to habituate ineffective practices? Did I fail to protect her from her criticizing herself too harshly?

I have been carrying this stone of an idea around in my pocket for many months, turning it over and over until my hands have worn it smooth and my fingers have memorized its surface. Even though I have been holding onto it tightly for a very long time now, I am still not confident that I will remember its details if I take it out of my pocket and put it somewhere to rest.

Instead of focusing on the 99 things that go well, I usually can find the one thing that didn't, particularly if I am looking at myself. However, if our efforts are 99% successful, they are noteworthy by any measure. The amazing thing is that I am beginning to learn that if 87%, 65%, or even 35% of our endeavors are successful, then these are where we should place our energy, rather than on the 13%, 35%, or even 65% of our endeavors that fail. Then we can study, replicate, and multiply the positive aspects of these undertakings. Regardless of the quantity, seeing the good in the work in which we and the teachers in our schools are engaged will contribute to continued growth far beyond that which comes from detailing their shortcomings and ours.

The implications of the "positive experience" question reach even farther. If we evaluate our work and teachers evaluate their work based on whether or not the experience was positive, then, because whatever outcome is measured is the outcome toward which we work, there will be more positive experiences throughout the school. If teachers have a positive experience when they work with us reflecting on and improving their practice, then they'll want to work with us to reflect on and improve their practice even more!

Of course, I know that it takes more than fun and love to teach a child to read, and it takes more than a positive experience for teachers to reflect and grow. Children can have a positive experience in "guided reading" when they cut pictures of things that begin with the letter *p* out of magazines and glue them to a sheet of "puh-puh-puh-paper." We have all known classrooms where the children have endless fun and are "in love" with their teacher, but there is little meaningful literacy work in the classroom.

However, if we are looking as hard as we can at a teacher's instructional delivery and we cannot find much—or maybe even anything—positive on which to build, we need to look again. Most of the time, guided reading instruction will at least resemble guided reading, even if only in one aspect. Then this one aspect is the first rung on a ladder of change. If the children have a positive experience, then, nine times out of 10, there are many appropriate and sound instructional practices in place. If children are in fact gluing p words, then the positive experience is still an opportunity for a coach to initiate a conversation with a teacher.

If after lengthy scrutiny a literacy coach still doesn't see anything positive, the problem is probably bigger than average, and the literacy coach is probably not the first to notice it. If administrators need our support in dealing with personnel or incompetence issues, they will let us know. If they don't, we should move on.

If we have expressed our concerns to our administrator and our efforts with the teacher continue to fail, we need to shift our focus. We could easily spend all our time in the most difficult classroom while other teachers, who would appreciate and benefit from our support, are working to solve problems without it. I am referring to extreme cases; I generally think literacy coaches need to work with every member of a school community in order to foster the whole community's growth. However, there are exceptions that can create barriers for everyone.

Perhaps some people find this positive experience stuff a little soft. Let me clarify: I am not talking about the larger evaluations of an entire schoolwide effort or determinations of which instructional models or strategies to adopt; these decisions must rest in research. Nor am I talking about camouflaging real work in the foliage of kindness. There is no way to skirt the challenge and the sweat associated with influencing instruction, particularly if it is done in a way that takes care of teachers. On the contrary, this work is harder than that of mandates and ultimatums because it requires a coach to focus on the teaching in the context of the teacher, and it demands a patient commitment to facilitating rather than demanding change.

Focusing on Teachers Rather Than Students

The idea of a coach focusing on teachers rather than students is not as radical as it may appear. I write of it while recognizing the risk of being misunderstood. This focus on teachers does not exclude scrutinizing student data to make decisions about instruction and to determine our level of effectiveness. It does not disregard the effectiveness of the practices teachers are implementing or the evaluation of the work of teachers and students based on qualitative and quantitative evidence of how well the students are reading and writing. However, the path of growth runs through rather than around the teachers. This is largely the philosophy of most literacy reform movements, on paper at least, although the focus on teachers may be articulated differently.

For example, Reading First legislation requires much testing and quantitative data collection. However, its description of the skills it requires of its coaches is primarily aimed at supporting teachers. For example, the United States government expects Reading First literacy coaches to "Look for the positive in each interactive opportunity" and "Display strong listening skills, questioning abilities, and confidentiality" (Learning Point Associates, 2004, p. 5). In fact, the list of the 16 qualifications of Reading First literacy coaches only includes one direct reference to students and many to teachers and staff.

Joyce and Showers (2002) use the term *student achievement* in their book, *Student Achievement Through Staff Development*, and their text lives up to its title. However, when you look at the practices presented in their work, it is apparent that Joyce and Showers put their energies into teachers and make a point of taking care of them. They write, "We focus on student achievement as *the product of formal study by educators—* study oriented directly toward improvements in curriculum and instruction and accompanied by continuous examination of student learning" (emphasis added, p. 3). Toward this end, the action they describe focuses on teachers. They further explain,

> Our proposition is that if a teacher or a community of teachers
> - engages, for a dozen days during the school year, in the formal study of curriculum or a teaching strategy that is useful across curriculum areas, and
> - regularly studies implementation and consequent student learning, then
> - the odds are that student achievement will rise substantially. (p. 3)

Joyce and Showers offer many other examples of how to take care of teachers so they can help students learn. From eliminating formal feedback to documenting the number of demonstrations a teacher needs to experience successful first attempts with a strategy, their work demonstrates an interest in empowering rather than excoriating teachers.

The benefits to coaching in this fashion reach beyond individual classrooms. In the end, helping the teachers feel safe and confident and positive not only affects instruction but also helps coaches feel safe and confident and positive. In relation to the positive experiences that can surround our work, Barkley and Bianco (2005) state, "A coaching relationship provides the opportunity for reciprocity of gifts of knowledge and skill, caring and support, feedback and celebration" (p. 5). A boomerang of support can develop in our schools and, when it returns to us, can make literacy coaching a positive experience for the coach, too.

Watching Teachers Teach

Early in my first year as a literacy coach, I tried to go into classrooms to watch teachers teach. I wanted to know what was happening in classrooms, and I was receiving a fair amount of encouragement from the administration to do so. However, I was not always sure how to most appropriately share feedback with teachers. They inevitably wanted to know if they had "done it right." I wanted to give them written feedback, and I wanted to meet with them individually. However, I was not sure how to structure either of these contexts.

One day a solution presented itself. A classroom teacher requested written feedback after I had been in her classroom and suggested that we have a school form. I reflected on this for a while and devised a form that I could fill out when I was in the classroom and give to teachers. I then piloted it in a few classrooms where it was met with a positive response.

The structure of the feedback form is simple. I record my name, the teacher's name, and the area of the literacy framework (e.g., writer's workshop, read-aloud, guided reading, working with words, or independent reading). I use the middle portion of the form to simply write an objective description of what the teacher and students are doing, focusing, when applicable, on the area of particular concern to the teacher. Finally, at the bottom of the form, there is an area for me to write comments (see Appendix). I staple this form to what usually includes many pages of scripting—that is, I write down as much as I can of what the teacher and the students say during my visit. This scripting then becomes a source of specific examples that the teacher and I can use when we are debriefing the lesson.

The words we choose to communicate with our teachers are absolutely critical. The nature of the feedback depends heavily on the nature of our relationship with the teacher. For the most part, my written (and spoken for that matter) feedback to teachers is positive. This is intentional and can, as discussed in the previous section, promote more growth than a detailed list of suggestions.

As literacy coaches support teachers thoughtfully and guide implementation of instructional strategies, they will inevitably see teachers working to make those strategies their own. Every time I go into classrooms, usually to follow up on something we have addressed in professional learning, I feel deeply respectful of teachers, so my positive reactions are sincere. I think that teachers know when they are being manipulated by praise and when feedback is genuine and in response to strong work. Consequently, we have to be intentional about developing the habit of noticing and appreciating what teachers do well *before* we try to figure out what they can do better. However, our ultimate goal is for teachers to observe their own strengths and promote their own reflection and growth. We must make sure teachers don't define themselves by our feedback.

This visitation feedback instrument has played a critical role in the school's growth in literacy instruction. It has accomplished a number of things for us. First, it has initiated conversations and opened lines of communication between teachers and me. Teachers want to grow more when they feel they have been successful. Next, it has helped me document my work and the growth of teachers. I give a copy of the form to teachers and keep a copy to serve as my anecdotal record of teacher growth. Finally, it has contributed positively to the cultures of professional learning and community in our school. Teachers expect and appreciate written feedback. Sometimes they even request that visitors to our school complete feedback forms after spending time in their classrooms. Figure 4 shows a sample of the written feedback I might offer after visiting a classroom.

Word Choices

Giving written and spoken feedback is an opportunity to be very thoughtful about the words we choose in communicating with teachers. This is a challenge. There are nuances to our word choices that we don't

Figure 4
Sample Classroom Visitation Feedback Form

CLASSROOM VISITATION FEEDBACK FORM

Visitor	Burkins							
Teacher	Wilson	Date	4-13-06	Time In	10:30	Time Out	11:00	

Lesson	Guided Reading		Writer's Workshop	X	Working With Words	
	Shared Reading		Independent Reading		Read-Aloud	
	Other					

What the students were doing	What the teacher was doing
Sitting on the rug, participating in the minilesson Moved to tables and self-selected work areas around the room. Writing on self-selected topics Moved back to rug to share work.	Presenting minilesson on what to do when you want to know how to spell a word Circulating and conferences with students about their writing. Keeping anecdotal records. Facilitating sharing.
Students: 16+2 (2 re-entered classroom from ESOL class at 10:40	Texts: NA

Impact on Learning and Instructional Considerations: David, you do much to encourage the independence of your students while also giving them the support they need to succeed. For example, you supported your students with their verbal rehearsal before they began writing. You also supported them as they changed one-word responses into complete sentences. I don't know if you realize it, but your responses are sophisticated and grounded in some strong research. Perhaps we have spoken about this before; you consistently repeat and expand on what students are saying. I saw a lot of independent behaviors from your students when they were trying to spell words in their independent writing. You reviewed classroom procedures for dealing with words (Continued)

Figure 4
Sample Classroom Visitation Feedback Form (continued)

CLASSROOM VISITATION FEEDBACK FORM

they didn't know, and you directed them to those procedures if they tried to get you to spell a word for them. They seem familiar with ways to use the tools in the classroom. Julio demonstrated this when he went to get the life cycle chart to use it to spell "motorcycle." You are teaching strategies rather than just giving your students finite information. This puts them in a position to teach themselves.

How are you connecting components of your writer's workshop? You might consider tying your conferences to the minilesson, thus reinforcing your students' use of the strategies demonstrated in the minilesson. However, the fact that your students didn't seem to need much support with ending punctuation in their independent writing may be an indication that they understood the minilesson well enough to apply the information. I think that you might "nudge" them to take their writing a little deeper by expanding their conversations before they begin to write. I'm not sure how practical this is in an ESOL setting. However, it might be worth experimenting with, and I would be happy to explore it with you.

always catch because we are looking through a different lens than the teacher. Choosing to focus primarily on strengths rather than weaknesses does not mean that we are insincere; it is "possible to be tactful without being inauthentic" (Loehr & Schwartz, 2003, p. 85). Although I am not always successful at avoiding words that are laced with inappropriate implications, I do, however, always work at it.

Showers and Joyce (1996) have investigated the thorniness of giving feedback. They developed a system for peer coaching that has been the supporting structure for the coaching we currently do. They choose to omit verbal feedback as a component of the observation process because it seemed to adversely affect collaboration.

When teachers try to give one another feedback, collaborative activity tends to disintegrate. Peer coaches told us they found themselves slipping into "supervisory, evaluative comments" despite their intentions to avoid them. Teachers shared with us that they expect "first the good news, then the bad" because of past experiences with clinical supervision, and admitted they often pressured their coaches to go beyond the technical feedback and give them "the real scoop." (p. 14)

Perkins (1998) studied the patterns of verbal feedback of inexperienced literacy coaches after they participated in a peer-coaching training workshop. The results provide insight into the problematic nature of this important aspect of coaching:

They more often asked closed-ended rather than open-ended questions, which, in turn imbued their statements with negative presuppositions. They paraphrased less and less frequently as their cycles progressed, and they used few probes to facilitate each other's cognition. Participants used evaluation, closed-ended questions, and negative presuppositions. Coaches conveyed identities as superior and inferior teachers, caretakers, and care-needers. Their talk revealed a lack of belief in the value of the communication and agenda skills. (p. 243)

Given the communication challenges implicit to coaching, coaches need to be deliberate in developing their coaching vocabularies because feedback skills require nurturing. Novice coaches usually don't enter the profession with deeply developed or efficient styles for offering feedback to teachers. The consequences of a coach's learning curve can be devastating, so we must work on the front end of change and view all communications from a proactive stance. New coaches are wise to begin humbly. Since collegial conversations and planning are as effective as feedback (Joyce & Showers, 2002), beginning coaches may choose to be slow to offer feedback. Communication is tricky, especially in relationships where we may suggest that someone change.

The nature of a coach's feedback will have a direct bearing on his relationship with a teacher and his circuitous effect on children. Guiney (2001) interviewed a classroom teacher, Helen O'Malley, about her experiences working with a literacy coach. O'Malley explains,

Initially I was sort of anxious because I was not quite sure what Charlotte's [literacy coach] role was going to be in my classroom.... I thought she was going to be there critiquing my lessons, saying to me, "We do this, this, and this in Writers' Workshop." And it hasn't been like that at all. It has just developed into a collegial relationship. Charlotte is there to reassure me, to guide me. She offers me suggestions, but she does so in a manner that enables me, half the time, to feel that I am coming up with these wonderful ideas. (p. 740)

We do all of these: We reassure. We guide. We suggest. We share ideas. Most important though, we measure our words in this work because if we are not careful, our words will become the yardstick by which teachers measure themselves. Following are a few things I have learned about what to say and what not to say to teachers in written and spoken feedback. As with everything in this book, these are developed around my paradigm and from my coaching perspective. Yours may be slightly or extremely different, and that is OK.

Giving thanks. One thing I have decided *not* to say to teachers is, "Thank you." I used to say, "Thank you for working so hard for your children," or "Thank you for preparing your lesson so thoroughly." As I began to think honestly about my choice of words, I was startled by my implications. First, I was saying that working hard for their children is not something teachers do anyway, but rather something they were doing for me. Second, I was placing my positive opinion as a subjective, extrinsic reward they could earn.

So now sometimes I say, "I appreciate your attention to the details of guided reading. Your sophistication in prompting your readers is teaching them independence." However, I use the word *appreciate* like I would say I appreciate a work of art or a bottle of wine, and I still use it sparingly.

Specificity communicates sincerity. Basically, if we are general with our feedback to teachers, they will have only a cloudy idea of the positive or not-so-positive areas of their work. If we are specific, they will be able to see clearly. Teachers will know that our words are "real and not empty flattery, and the evidence is in the details" and the way we share them with teachers (Johnston, 2004, p. 38).

If I tell a teacher that she is "good" I am not only making a value judgment, I am also communicating that I can't quite put my finger on what makes her good. Instead I will say, "You are organized, attentive to your children's emotional needs, and knowledgeable about the reading process." Then I will cite specific examples from my notes that support these statements. Rather than saying, "I like the way you introduced the book," I will say, "Your book introduction was comprehensive, and you made choices that facilitated your students' later success with the text. For example...."

Making judgment calls. In the previous section, I referred to the word *good* as a value judgment. There are other words that convey value judgments such as *nice*, *like*, and *love*. I don't think that these words are absolute mustn'ts. I do think, however, that we should use them sparingly and in selective contexts.

For example, if we say, "I love the way you talk to your children," it is very different from saying, "I love those magic markers," or "I love the book you read." The difference is that one statement passes judgment on the teacher, and the others pass judgment on things. A better statement about teacher–student communication would be, "The way you talk to your children makes it safe for them to take risks and demonstrates that you value them as individuals. For example, you said...." Then I would list—verbatim when my notes allowed—statements the teacher made that illustrate my point.

Like is another dangerous word in the context of teacher feedback. If we are going to talk about what we *like*, we must be sure to communicate that these are our opinions. Usually when a coach says he likes something, it means that the coach thinks the teacher should like the same thing. It is a subtle direction. For example, if a teacher is employing round-robin methods for listening to children read their books in guided reading, a coach might say, "I like to let everyone read at the same time and then lean in and listen to one child at a time." If you say something like this, you might follow it with something like, "...but that is just my preference." A better option is to say something like, "I see that you manage to listen to every child read in guided reading. This practice in instructional level text will support their growth as readers. You might consider letting them all read at once, while you listen to one at a time. Research demonstrates that this increases the total reading time of each child and minimizes inattentive behaviors because...."

We have to give teachers room to disagree, and their disagreement has to be OK with us. Often, feeling "wrong" will push teachers into an emotional space that will interfere with their growth. Besides, we coaches don't know everything. Is it an impossibility that next month a study could come out that indicates that there are significant, measurable benefits to round-robin reading? We must be careful what we declare absolute, because such declarations end further conversation.

The "leading edge." Johnston has written an entire book about the subtleties of our communications. In *Choice Words: How Our Language Affects Children's Learning* (2004), Johnston references Clay's (1993) work and explores the places where we are partially correct. He writes, "This leading edge is where the student has reached beyond herself, stretching what she knows just beyond its limit, producing something that is partly correct. This is the launching pad for new learning" (p. 13). This means that as we are focusing on what teachers are doing well, we are also looking for the places where they are doing part of something well or doing something partially well. We need to notice when their success brings about learning opportunities. These are the corners of learning where skill and risk meet. Such corners provide us the opportunity to both teach and celebrate, and when we point them out, teachers have the opportunity to see at what point their stretching has, in fact, extended their reach. In addition, when a teacher is partially correct, it means that soon he will have another success. Furthermore, if we teach teachers the strategy of recognizing "failed" attempts as partially correct and then analyzing their correctness, we set in motion a self-reflective process.

Naming the interactions. Again, in the context of observations, I find myself scrutinizing my word choices. I do fewer and fewer *observations*, and I make more and more *classroom visits*. I spend less time *observing* and more time *watching*. No matter how you couch it, conducting an *observation* is threatening. Making a *visit* to a classroom is safer. *Watching* is less threatening than *observing*. I never use the word *evaluation*. *Evaluation* should be an inaccurate description of our work, and it is tainted by authority's influence.

I say that I am using the words *observation* and *observing* less and less because a shift in primary vocabulary takes effort and conscious practice. We first have to decide that *watching* is a better word than *observing*. Then we have to decide to try to amend our speech to adopt this substitution. The next step, the hardest step, is having to *notice* when we are using the word we have targeted for change. Then we have to correct ourselves. This process is gradual and is a reflection of any process of developing or breaking a habit.

Measuring Our Words

Subtexts are by definition subtle, and I'm not always successful at communicating effectively. To help facilitate explorations of word choice, Table 3 shows examples of effective feedback in the form of sentences and sentence stems. A parallel nonexample for each item can be found in the right-hand column. I do not offer these as an exhaustive reference but rather as a series of examples to search for patterns, shape into strategies, and explore intentionally through interactions with teachers and others.

These sentences and stems are not absolutes; there may be contexts where it is absolutely appropriate to say a teacher is "good." There may also be times when you actually do know what is best, and it is appropriate to tell a teacher what you think is best. On the other hand, we shouldn't be shackled by the fear that our words are communicating ideas we didn't intend. My intent is not for coaches to feel restricted but to feel free to work even more productively with teachers.

Making the Rounds: Visiting Everyone

Anyone who knows me would say that I have a "Type A" personality. In some situations this has served me well, in others it has made life complicated. I am constantly trying to balance my need to be systematic against an effort to avoid being too rigid. However, being systematic has its benefits. For example, dentists tell us that when we brush our teeth, we should be systematic about it. We should start at the lower back on one side, moving to the other side, then moving up and across the top teeth. Also, we should attend to all the surfaces of our teeth (front, back, top, and sides) in a systematic way. If we don't, the eventual state of our teeth will betray our inadvertent brushing patterns. Brushers who are not systematic will unintentionally brush in the same pattern daily and, consequently, miss the same spots every time. This is analogous to teachers unwittingly calling on children sitting in certain areas of the classroom more than others.

Developing systems to prevent leaving something or someone out is insurance against our natural inclination to work in patterns. For

Table 3
Examples and Nonexamples of Effective Feedback

We need to explore how to...	*You* need to figure out how to... (unsupportive; blaming)
I can tell that you have been working on _____ because...	You did a *good* job with... (vague, value judgment)
Students in this group are strong in... What is your next priority for them?	Students in this group really *need* to focus on... (Offers your opinion as absolute fact and suggests instructional weakness and/or inattention.)
Your students have progressed to the point that they may be ready to use the pictures and the print to figure out the words on their own during reading. You might consider pulling back some, now that they have developed the skills to support their work.	*Let* your students figure out the words during reading. Don't tell them the words. (Implies that the teacher has been inhibiting the progress of the children and that the coach knows best.)
Students seem proud of their achievement and are beginning to solve problems as they read. You might consider encouraging them to...	Your students are figuring out words *but* they are not cross-checking. You really *need* to teach them to... (Implies that the teacher hasn't been teaching them or that what she has been teaching was not appropriate.)
What are your priorities for your professional growth and how can I help you reach them?	*I'm* here to help you *improve* in ... (*Improve* implies shortcomings or deficiencies and is a moving target. Statement places the coach in a position of superiority.)
Your instruction is powerful because research has indicated that when teachers...	I *love* the way you teach. (vague, value judgment)
Your students are demonstrating balanced strategy use. This is an indication that you are giving them balanced instruction.	Your students are *good* readers. *Thank you* for teaching them so carefully. (condescending and vague)
You might consider trying _____ when you are helping children with a difficult and phonetically irregular word like "through."	It's *not a good idea* to say, "Who can tell me the word?" especially when the word is difficult and phonetically irregular like *through*. (negative value judgment)
I enjoyed watching you model developmental spelling today. In my opinion, developmental spelling makes sense because...and it seemed particularly effective in this context.	I *liked* the way you used invented spelling when you were modeling drafting. (Invites teacher dependence on coach to decide "right" way to teach.)

example, I have a plan for getting around to all the classrooms in my school. In the past, I have made detailed schedules to make sure I get into every classroom to see every component of the literacy framework. However, this year I have used a much simpler system. I just have a form with teacher names on the top and framework elements down the side, as illustrated in Figure 5. Then I simply write the date in the box when I observe a particular instructional model in a classroom.

Getting Into Classrooms

Coaches may find, however, that keeping a record of the classrooms they have visited may be much easier than getting into those classrooms in the first place. Thus far, this chapter has addressed ways to communicate with teachers in response to watching their lessons and how to avoid overlooking pockets of instruction in a school. However, one of the biggest challenges for most coaches is simply getting into the classroom.

Getting invited into a classroom is a lot like getting invited (or not getting invited) to a party, and sometimes it's just as awkward and stressful. There are basically three ways to get through classroom doors to watch lessons. However, I don't think that a coach should use one of these methods exclusively. It is the combination of the three that rounds out our work in classrooms.

Crashing the party. The first method for getting into a party is "crashing." Visiting someone's classroom without an invitation is analogous to crashing a party. Most coaches have the option of just dropping into a teacher's classroom unannounced. However, there are implications to this that we need to consider.

When I began coaching, the field was in its infancy. I was whittling the shape of my work. At the time, however, there weren't many resources on coaching to support my work. I began my classroom observations by dropping into classrooms unannounced. Unannounced visits to classrooms imbue us with the power that is inherent in having the authority to walk into someone else's classroom without telling or asking them, staying in the room and observing for as long as we want, and then responding to what we have seen and interpreted as a priority. Barkley and Bianco (2005) write, "in a school setting if a 'coach' walks in

Figure 5
Sample Classroom Visitation Record

	Allison	Jill	Dana	Susan	Ben	Vicki	Karen
Read-Aloud	9/27	8/12	10/22 1/18		9/13	12/06	
Shared Reading	8/10	8/01 1/06					
Guided Reading	9/16	8/04 10/28	11/17	4/19	11/20	9/17 10/27	10/27
Independent Reading	10/10	11/14 4/03		8/22 12/09 1/24	10/10		11/20
Reader's Workshop	1/31 2/11	11/09	9/20	11/05 4/18		8/15 9/09	8/15
Model Writing	10/20 4/22	10/05		9/07 2/16 3/12			
Shared Writing	9/07		11/14	9/29	1/11	10/12	
Writer's Workshop	9/01		8/02	10/21		2/27 3/9 3/15 4/17	11/20
Journal Writing		9/13	8/03	9/30	8/30		
Word Work	11/07	8/14	11/28 12/04	8/14		11/20 2/28	
Other	9/17	8/12 2/7		10/10 3/6	2/14	1/18	

to observe a classroom unannounced and uninvited, it's not coaching. It's evaluation or supervision" (p. 105).

Unannounced visits give teachers little or no choice, and the degree of choice is a measure of power. Coaches have the choice to go into any classroom at any time, and teachers have little choice once we get there. I am speaking in the extreme; I certainly honor a teacher who says, "Today is just a really bad day." But no matter how we look at it, dropping in on teachers places coaches in a power role.

Without fully realizing what I was doing, I used this expression of authority for a couple of years before I even learned of other options. I'm still not really comfortable with drop-in visits; however, district and school administrators expect me to do this. The teachers and I have been able to make this system work, as well as I think we can, by keeping the lines of communication open and by honoring each other as people. However, there are at least two other ways for a coach to get into classrooms, and both are probably better than dropping in uninvited.

Receiving an invitation. The best way to be included in a party is to receive a sincere, legitimate invitation. In parallel, the best way to get into a classroom is for a teacher to invite you. After two years of coaching, I was officially "trained" to be a coach, and I learned of the coaching model described by Lyons and Pinnell in *Systems for Change in Literacy Education: A Guide to Professional Development* (2001). As I researched *Coaching For Balance*, I learned that this model is not new and has been used in a number of contexts (DuFour, 2002; Garmston, Linder, & Whittaker, 2003; McAllister & Neubert, 1995). Partly out of my continued discomfort with dropping in on teachers and partly out of my obligation to complete my assignments for my own professional learning, I began utilizing this system.

So I started to wait for teachers to invite me before I visited their classrooms. I put a sign-up schedule on my office door. I invited teachers to invite me into their classrooms. Then I waited. I applied some gentle pressure with e-mails like, "In order for you to get professional learning credit for this summer's writing workshop professional learning, you will need to have two classroom visits. So come see me if you would like me to take care of these for you." Needless to say, teachers weren't running over one another in a mad dash to my office door. The "sign-up" pen never ran out of ink.

There were some teachers who signed up. Some I believe needed, in all honesty, professional learning credit. Others really had areas they wanted support for changing. Some, I think, felt sorry for me.

Then, of course, there was the difficulty associated with having a calendar for signing up on my door and another calendar that I carried around with me. I began overextending myself and, sometimes, double-booking myself. I found myself sitting in the hall in front of my door copying times and names into my travel calendar. Eventually I e-mailed teachers that I was taking the sign-up sheet off my door but that I was still eager to be invited into their classrooms.

Meanwhile I worked through the coaching cycles with those who, for one reason or another, had asked me to visit their classrooms. The preconference–observation–postconference cycle proved very gratifying for me and, based on their responses, for teachers. The cycle truly gives ownership of the process to teachers, which is where it should be. Teachers decide when we will visit, what we will see, why we are visiting, and what they want to hear from us. We limit the work to that which teachers expressly request. Overall, it is a sound, enriching, stretching process that I highly endorse.

The disadvantage of waiting to get invited into classrooms is that some, perhaps even many, teachers won't invite us in. This isn't necessarily because teachers don't like us or don't want us in their classrooms. Often times, it is just a matter of time. Even when teachers are absolutely comfortable with us watching them teach, inviting us into their rooms involves examining their schedule, considering what they would be teaching, communicating with us, returning to the schedule, and so forth. What some might argue is a negligible amount of time, in the context of classrooms and relative to the "free time" teachers do have, is actually quite a lot. And after all the deliberation, most teachers who are truly comfortable with us in their rooms will say, "Just come in any time." Then we are back to dropping in.

Inviting yourself. I once wanted to attend a party to which my best friend was invited, but I was not, and I asked my friend to get me invited. The coaching equivalent to this is planning our visits but letting the teachers know when we are coming and what we are interested in seeing. This affords coaches the opportunity to see the instructional areas they think most pressing, which is a challenge when we drop by unannounced. Planned visits also give teachers a say in decision making. If a teacher finds the time a coach has scheduled to visit his classroom inconvenient, he can let the coach know and they can reschedule the visit together.

As a happy medium, announced visits have worked for me. I feel less like I am intruding, I see a teacher's instructional best, and I make better use of my time in the classroom. One way I have scheduled these visits has been to select an instructional area, such as read-aloud. Then I communicate with teachers that I will be visiting everyone in the next two weeks to watch read-aloud, and I ask them if they have a time they would like me to visit their rooms. Finally, I develop and distribute a schedule. Teachers come to me with conflicts, and we work around them. I stick to the subject of the visit; I don't go in to watch read-aloud and then offer suggestions about writer's workshop. This system has proven effective, particularly as a complement to the other two visitation options.

Souvenirs

Our words can be a scaffold or an impediment. We need to recognize the limitations of our language, and we need to understand how our communications influence the work of teachers. One avenue for developing our coaching vocabularies and encouraging teacher growth is through visiting classrooms to watch instruction and engaging in follow-up discussions. Classroom visits provide us with a valuable way to both understand the learning phase through which a teacher is working and to individualize our support. However, they require sensitivity to layers of need involving content and emotion. If we want teachers to want to work with us, we cannot spend most of our time talking about what they are not doing. We must train ourselves to hone in on the positive aspects of a teacher's work and use those strengths to support their extensions of their own learning.

CHAPTER 8

Assessment Literacy: Learning to Make Sense of Data

"It is the spirit of the age to believe that any fact, no matter how suspect, is superior to any imaginative exercise, no matter how true."
Gore Vidal, *United States: Essays 1952–1992*, 1993, p. 98

Educators speak often of data-driven instruction. In a larger sense, we should think of our data-driven lives. We are constantly gathering data from our world and trying to reconcile them or let them tell a story. Generally speaking, most of our actions are defined through, guided by, and evaluated against some form of data. In our daily lives, data are not intimidating.

When my son explains to me that his teacher told him not to do any math practice because it would make him too tired, I analyze data that give me qualitative insight into my son's love–hate relationship with mathematics. His report card and notes from his teacher give me the quantitative information to back up my earlier analyses. Human beings are statistics in motion, ably supported by a brain that is hungry for patterns. For this reason, we can think of data analysis as a coat we slip into comfortably, or perhaps the pair of eyeglasses we misplace on our own heads and which we just need someone to remind us we are already wearing.

The Marriage of Qualitative and Quantitative Data

In the work of school change, data are our allies. All of our decision making should and does—whether we realize it or not—evolve from data analysis. Whether we are considering topics for the next professional learning session or helping teachers decide what kind of paper to order for first grade, we are constantly considering data.

In my professional and scholastic life, I have encountered people who argue the relative values of quantitative and qualitative data. Once again, balance is our ally. The most valuable data, I think, are in the places where quantitative and qualitative information overlap. If what we are noticing in classrooms is supported by numbers, then we have some confidence that, because we are utilizing multiple perceptions, what we think we are seeing isn't all in our heads. If we think we are observing one thing but the numbers are telling us something different, then we need more information. If the numbers conflict with rather than align with our observations, we need to continue questioning.

Although there are trends among researchers to favor either qualitative or quantitative data, we don't make informed decisions by eliminating entire disciplines of data analysis and their respective data pools. We do become informed by looking into as many data sets, whether pools or puddles, as we reasonably can and by letting our brains search out the patterns they are naturally inclined to find.

Imagine that the library circulation in a coach's school increases dramatically over a particular period of time. He may begin to speculate about the reasons so that, upon discovering the cause, he can do more of a good thing. He may compare library circulation levels by classroom to the same class's growth in the context of guided reading. Did measures demonstrate that the same children who checked out the most books made the most growth in reading ability?

If the data are really compelling, and he is really curious, he may administer some kind of student survey about independent reading. He will gather qualitative data from the librarian and her assistant, asking them if they have observed any trends in student reading motivation or if they have ideas about what may have caused the increase in circulation. If the information is available, he may see if there is a correlation between children whose parents read with them every night and the children who check out the most books.

Although data are invaluable in making instructional decisions, we need to proceed with caution. The original research question can take us in more directions than we are able or willing to go. It often grows so many branches that we could spend all of our time trying to climb to the uppermost branch of the hypothesis tree while our coaching work waits below on the ground. We have to decide how far we are willing to climb and at what point we need to turn around and climb down.

A Data Story: What Data Can Reveal

During my first year administering reading inventories at my school, we used federal funds to hire six people to test the children. The advantage of this was that it was easier to achieve consistency with six people than it would have been with 25. Also, instructional time wasn't spent administering assessments. I really wanted our data to be reliable so we would have a true picture of whether our efforts were affecting the literacy levels of our students. When every teacher in your school is administering an assessment, there is added opportunity for variation in protocol and interpretation.

The disadvantage of external evaluators administering reading inventories, of course, is that teachers miss the opportunity to learn about their children as readers. In an effort to resolve this issue, we used digital tape recorders to record all the readers and saved the recordings to a shared drive that teachers could access. We also gave the teachers the scored forms to compare to the readings. These recordings also proved very helpful when someone in the group of test administrators had a case where the data were unclear. Perhaps a child jumped from independent reading level on one text to frustration level on the very next text. We were then able to listen to the recordings as a group and reach a shared conclusion.

In our second year implementing a balanced literacy framework, we didn't administer reading inventories in the fall. We didn't have the funds to hire independent proctors, and I didn't feel I would have time to train teachers to do it well in the limited amount of time I had with them at the beginning of the year. In the winter of our second year, we hired proctors again. I trained them, and they tested the whole school.

However, because we had no baseline data from the fall, we couldn't find out what kind of progress children had made. This was unfortunate, and I learned a critical lesson through this experience. Data don't just serve to validate a program; they serve to validate the work of teachers and provide cause for celebrations. Legitimate celebration is critical to morale, which in our case suffered because of our lack of data. Fortunately, because one data pool can provide different pictures of students and teachers, there were other ways to uncover positive stories in the data that then supported our celebrations even though we did not have pre- and posttest information.

What we were able to assess was our ability to determine a guided reading level for children. Teachers had placed children in the fall based on the results of their spring benchmarks and then made adjustments based on their qualitative judgments about how well the children read at a given level. How accurate were our qualitative judgments about placing children in instructional level text? When we erred, did we err toward more difficult texts or easier texts? Were the children more likely to be in books that were too difficult, too easy, or just right for them?

I have consistently observed that students reading from books that are difficult for them are likely to become stuck and often develop poor reading habits that also interfere with their progress. A child who demonstrated efficient use of the cueing systems at a Level H but was taught in a Level J was likely to get stuck while also developing, possibly solidifying, the inefficient habit of overrelying on one cueing system or another. It was not unusual for such a child to demonstrate on the second benchmark less skill than she had on the first.

On the other hand, I have often seen children make tremendous progress working in books that were manageable for them. For example, a child who benchmarked a Level G but was reading in a Level E text might manage to read a Level J when retested, thus demonstrating growth through levels in which she was never instructed. Based on my school's modest but consistent quantitative and qualitative data, I encouraged teachers to err down in levels if they had doubts about placement or if they had to adjust text levels to accommodate other members of a group.

Table 4	
Percent of Students Instructed On, Above, and Below Instructional Level	
Students who could be moved to more challenging text	54%
Students needing to be moved to easier text	13%
Students working in "just right" text	33%

Our winter benchmark data illustrated how well teachers had applied this information. Because I wanted to make sure that the data were accurate, I reviewed every benchmark record and received clarification from the test administrators where I needed it. Once the data were collected I studied them. I compared the levels where children were being taught to the levels at which, on benchmark record, they demonstrated proficiency. As I usually do, I compiled these data and organized them to present to the entire faculty. Table 4 illustrates what the data revealed.

I was excited about these data because they meant that teachers had heard and understood what I had explained to them. They meant that, when teachers weren't sure where to place students for guided reading, they were more likely to match them with text that was easy for them than into text that is "challenging." The data also illustrated that only 13% of our students were working from texts that were likely to develop inefficiency in the students' use and integration of reading strategies. Upon further investigation, I learned that more than half of the students working below their instructional level were working in texts that were only one level below their benchmarked instructional level.

So we were able to celebrate teacher skill at qualitatively assessing reading level and in erring down rather than up. It is worth the time to go to the data to search for indicators of positive trends as well as patterns of need. Even if the data are dismal, you are likely to find something worth noticing as positive. The stories that data tell us are the trail a school can follow to increasingly strong literacy instruction.

"Reliable" Assessments Aren't Always Reliable

Assessments can give the illusion of reliability, especially standardized tests. There is, I think, a negative correlation between replicability and the amount of information we can get from a test. The tests that are more subjective, such as reading inventories, give us more information. Tests that are more standardized generally offer, in my opinion, less specific data to guide instruction, although they aren't completely without value.

With the assessments literacy coaches administer, we need to try to strike a balance between reliability and specificity. However, no test is absolutely replicable nor is any test specific enough to give us absolutely dependable information about the processes that are taking place in the heads of children as they read. Consequently, the two sources of information must be weighed against each other.

Test administrations can vary in a myriad of ways. Even the temperature of the room can affect how well students perform on tests. Often, norm-referenced tests create an illusion of reliability that is convincing enough for them to serve as the sole measure on which policymakers rely to decide whether educators are effective or not. Test reliability, though, is often farther out of our reach than we realize.

Consequently, we have to go to great lengths to achieve consistency in assessment administration. The quality of our decisions rests heavily on the quality of our data, so the time we spend planning our data collection and teaching teachers how to administer assessments will save us time and spare us misinformation later. Little is more discouraging for a school than discovering it has been celebrating inaccurate data. For this reason, we must look for patterns in the data that are strong enough to give us a margin of error in our interpretations. We are wise to plan assessments carefully, analyze data thoughtfully, and view all data with suspicion.

Warning: The Data We Collect Influence the Instruction in Our Schools

If you are a potential publisher and you tell me you prefer professional books to be written in an academic voice, depending on how desperate I am, I may decide to pay special attention to this aspect of my manuscript before I send it to you. On the other hand, if you tell me you like a relaxed, conversational style in the books you publish, I will relax a little, too. Given that I can only attend to a few details in my writing at once, an editor's preference may influence how I choose which details deserve my attention.

Similarly, the data we request from teachers will influence how they decide which areas of their instruction on which to focus. For example, if a coach tells teachers that he is interested in collecting data on students' spelling skills and strategies, then teachers will probably be particularly thoughtful and deliberate about their spelling instruction. The coach will further affect teachers' decision making and focus by requesting specific information. If the coach specifically expresses interest in how well students spell high-frequency words in particular, then high-frequency words will probably get heavy attention during spelling instruction. If the coach says he is interested in how well students spell in their connected writing, then spelling in context might receive special attention.

This response from teachers isn't necessarily a reflection of the coach's influence. Instead, I think it is a reflection of our fear in general of failure and the behavioristic management structure that is common in education. Regardless of the reason, coaches need to be selective when soliciting data from teachers.

Early on as a coach, I found it useful to collect data on guided reading levels at the end of each month. Although there is value in collecting guided reading data with some regularity, I learned of some pretty significant consequences. If we collect guided reading levels, we run the risk of teachers feeling pressure and focusing on levels rather than reading behaviors. This may lead teachers to rush children through the levels and move them into higher text by offering increasing levels of scaffolding rather than because of demonstrated improvement in their reading.

It can be disastrous for a school to end up with a large population of children in books that are inappropriate for them in big and little ways. Even if we do manage to get students back into a place of appropriate reading comfort and challenge, we will be faced with the tremendous task of breaking the bad habits they have acquired while trying to cope with material that is too difficult for them.

In collecting the guided reading data, I frequently said to teachers, "This is not a race. We expect our students to progress, and they will, but don't move your students into more difficult text unless you are comfortable in the knowledge that it is appropriate for them." I have said this so many times that I am certain that a visitor could ask any of my teachers about the reports and they would reiterate what has been my mantra: "Don't push students through the levels."

Predictably, many students still ended up in texts that were too difficult for them. Furthermore, increasing reading levels became the central focus of our guided reading instruction. I wanted teachers to instead focus on developing strong reading behaviors that students could exercise in a number of reading levels. I wanted teachers to understand that if they gave students opportunities to practice balanced reading strategies, they would make progress, even if the level was lower than the maximum challenge they could handle.

How we began to shift our attention from levels to reading behaviors is a different story, but the decision to do so grew from a realization that the data I was collecting were negatively affecting the learning of teachers and the progress of students. I decided to collect guided reading levels only three times per year, when we benchmark students. We now summarize reading levels with a range ("She's working in a C–E range") rather than with one definitive level ("She's working on Level E"), and we also collect data on word-recognition percentages, depth of comprehension, and fluency.

Through the discussion surrounding these changes, we also decided that student progress through reading levels didn't necessarily have to be linear. Sometimes a student who is able to read from a Level N is better able to practice a new skill, learn a new genre, or practice fluency in a Level L. Sometimes a book labeled as a Level O reads more like a Level Q. These milestones in our learning have, of course, affected classroom instruction in our school.

I once heard of a school district that actually told its teachers that it expected the students to move up a guided reading level each month. Decisions such as this bring with them predictable repercussions, and children pay the price. Not only do we end up with teachers focusing on and rushing children through levels, we also end up with parents who are pushing their children through levels as well as pressuring the teachers.

Following are some thoughts for you to consider as you try to make wise decisions about data collection and interpretation in your school.

Change is continuous and bears on the relevance of particular assessments. When we first began teaching guided reading, we clung to guided reading levels like an inexperienced swimmer clings to an inner tube. They were for us the simplification of the very complicated process of matching books to readers. They were necessary water wings for us to stay afloat while we were in the initiating phases of guided reading. So this was a logical and appropriate place for us to begin our data collection.

As previously described, after guided reading became increasingly automatic and more and more teachers were moving into the culminating and inventing phases, we began to reexamine our reliance on levels. We learned that what were important data for us at one point in our change process became less important for us at later points. We began to shift our focus to the reading behaviors and reading processes of our students. As coaches, we are the key people in recognizing the need to facilitate a change in data focus, and we are usually the people to initiate and support the change. We do not need to keep an assessment just because it is a tradition in our school or district. We need to consider whether the data collected are still helpful given the current levels of skill and understanding across our school and the patterns of reading behavior across our school.

Schools regularly produce authentic data beyond assessments. Data collection doesn't have to be a monstrous undertaking or take place in a fabricated context. Gathering data is an integral part of much of the work in schools, whether those collecting the data realize it or not. My observations of how teachers respond during professional learning sessions are a data set. Teacher self-evaluations, running records, library circulation, PTA sign-in sheets, and attendance records are all data sets a coach can explore.

The key, of course, is using the most informative and relevant data. Schools need to connect to their work the abundance of data they possess. Lashway (1998) writes, "School personnel collect a prodigious amount of information, from test scores to attendance figures, yet rarely link this wealth of data to school-improvement efforts" (p. 1). Literacy coaches can play a valuable role in wisely employing data to identify questions and track the evidence that can answer them.

For example, what is the correlation between attendance rate and reading proficiency? What about the correlation between book checkout and parent involvement? Many tasks woven throughout our work can provide us with valuable information about the children's progress, and that of our own. The challenge becomes the identification of the most valuable data sets and the most productive routes of analysis.

Teachers give instructional priority to areas that are measured. The data collected influence the instruction in the school. We know this to be true for "high-stakes" tests. Certainly most schools make a priority of teaching the content that will be on these formal assessments.

Perhaps this phenomenon exists because any reporting feels evaluative, and teachers are concerned that they will be judged along the data collected. Perhaps it is because collecting the data brings to their attention an instructional need. Whatever the reason, the implications on a coach's work are sizeable, so we must be very thoughtful when we ask teachers to share data with us. It's like telling your family that you want to start collecting figurines of unicorns. Once your six aunts, four uncles, and 17 cousins learn of your new hobby, you may soon find yourself the guardian of an immense glass menagerie that rivals the china collection at the Smithsonian Art Museum in Washington, DC. Coaches must be careful what they ask for; sometimes requests come with unanticipated responses.

Celebration builds momentum. While negative trends typically stand out, it is worth searching for positive trends. For example, What percentage of students in the school read on "grade level"? Is it more than it was last year at this time? Are those who are behind closer than they were? Are our students who have been with us over a period of years doing better than those who have come in the middle of their elementary school careers? Is there evidence that almost everyone is teaching guided reading effectively? There is always something to celebrate in these data sets.

Coaches must make it a priority to find and celebrate positive data trends. As Baylor (1986) eloquently tells us in the title of his work, we are "in charge of celebrations." I first realized this as a parent trying to establish holiday traditions with my family. Festivity doesn't just materialize because of a date on a calendar; it comes from someone actively pursuing it. There's work represented in our holiday tables, and there will be work represented in your data and the celebration they authenticate. Even a modest success brings with it hope, and hope is a ladder on which teachers can climb.

Objective Data Facilitate Change

People generally need to have a reason to change. Big change is frightening, and we are all leery of failure and the devastating effects it has on our sense of worth. The emotion surrounding the reason to change has to be stronger than the fear surrounding the prospect of change. Some of the most powerful tools we have at our disposal are data. If a coach has put forth a vision for literacy in the school and communicated that it is sound, doable, practical, valuable, and most of all, capable of yielding results, then he must let the data speak. Often, what they have to say is hard to hear. Sometimes, we have to allow teachers "to feel the pinch of reality in order to stimulate them to adapt" (Heifetz & Laurie, 1997, p. 132).

A few weeks after I began working as a coach, we had a schoolwide meeting about literacy. In the weeks prior, I had been studying our data. I analyzed them along several variables. I looked for the hard stories they told. I tried to eliminate any arguments against the data. I asked these questions: What percentage of our students read on grade level? How far behind are the strugglers? What about our African American population? Our Hispanic population? Our special education students? Had students who had been with us since kindergarten done better than those who were more transient?

The results were startling, and I knew they would be difficult for the teachers to consider. When teachers have worked in a struggling school for a long time, many of them develop a defense mechanism in regard to the data. They have to; it's a survival skill. They are like doctors who can't get too close to their patients because of the risk of heartbreak.

Teachers in schools where a large percentage of children are not developing proficiency in reading often have a removed sense that things are not good. Probably, they have had people telling them for a while that they aren't "good" teachers or that they don't care. Perhaps they have had negative media coverage or reprimands from the district office.

Sometimes teachers will put much energy into explaining data rather than listening to the very hurtful things they are saying. But denial is an uncomfortable chair to sit in, hard-bottomed and straight-backed, and teachers usually welcome the comfort that honesty brings with it and the hope that comes from getting up and getting moving. That is what makes this data presentation different from others; coaches can offer teachers some hope.

Coaches must demonstrate respect when they present difficult data. They must step back and give the data and the faculty an opportunity to be honest with each other. Our first meeting about data was challenging. It brought home the fact that far too many of the students in our school were not learning to read. The data made it obvious that current practices were not effectively meeting the needs of our students. They eliminated the argument that the difficulties were only along certain racial or socioeconomic lines. The effect was sobering for the teachers because they all cared tremendously about the children they taught. Despite the discomfort, they did the hard thing: They took ownership of the problem and rallied to solve it.

This data investigation and its companion presentation were delicate, even potentially thorny. I wanted to reassure the teachers but also to let the discomfort with the data solidify their commitment to making the big changes that only come from difficult realizations. However, if there was too much discomfort, I knew I would run the risk of pushing teachers to a place that is too uncomfortable to stay in long enough to compose a portrait of change. I had to both push and protect. Teachers had a right to see the truth even if it was hard, as do the teachers in every school. Their reassurance came from working with a coach who let them know she had a plan and reminded them of this as a counterpoint to their discomfort.

Learning that we have some responsibility in a situation that has not been ideal for the children about whom we care profoundly can be heartbreaking. Some teachers seemed to work through an entire grieving process, moving from denial to anger and eventually to acceptance. The grief associated with difficult data is something that needs to run its course; coaches must respect it and step out of the way. Such experiences are extremely personal and sensitive, and I was not presumptuous enough to push my way into the teachers' emotional spaces. I gave them time, room, and when they demonstrated a readiness for it, support for moving in the direction of our vision.

Evaluating Ourselves

To a great extent, the most informative assessment of a coach's work is the progress of the children and the growth of the teachers. If things are not improving enough for the coach, and possibly others, to notice, he needs to closely examine the course of action behind and before him. The degree of progress will vary based on the school culture, the availability of resources, the coaching context, the professional learning history of the teachers, and the skill of the administrator. However, coaches should recognize changes even if they are simply shifts in the school culture or growth in relationships with teachers, changes that are not "simple" at all.

One valuable way for us to appraise our work is to look into the mirror of instruction in our schools. In most cases, teachers will replicate with accuracy the instruction we model for them. If we show teachers something new, they are likely to do what we teach them, even if it is not what we thought we taught.

If I model a first-grade guided reading lesson for a novice teacher and I use magnetic letters to reinforce the teaching point, then that teacher might include magnetic letters in her definition of guided reading from that point on unless she is exposed to something different through conversation, observation, or reading. For better or for worse, the work of teachers is often a reflection of the work of coaches. Effective coaches, like effective teachers, evaluate their instruction based on the demonstrated understandings of the student. The instruction in our schools is the most honest feedback on our work we will ever receive.

In addition to studying our reflections in the work of teachers, there are more strategic ways for a coach to gather feedback on her work. As a first-year coach, I was very interested in the progress of our students and valued the data as an indicator of the success of my work; however, I solicited more direct and specific information about how the teachers felt about the job I was doing as their literacy coach. So I developed a feedback form for teachers to complete and return to me anonymously (see Appendix).

The feedback form focused primarily on relationships. I wanted to know if the teachers felt like our working relationships were growing. This gave me interesting data to support the impressions I had of our first year working together. I also wanted to know if teachers felt like our professional learning sessions had been productive and valuable for them.

In addition to the feedback I pursued, I began to notice and collect unsolicited evaluations. These are the pieces of information we get from teachers and administrators that tell us they think our work is effective. When a teacher hugs me and says, "Thank you," that is an unsolicited evaluation. When a child writes me a poem, it is also an unsolicited evaluation. Unsolicited evaluations can be positive or negative, but I encourage coaches to cling tightly to the positive evaluations.

In the last year, I have had three teachers come to me and say that they want to pursue graduate degrees in literacy. This, for me, was an unsolicited evaluation. I took this to mean that they had enjoyed learning about literacy at our school and that they wanted to study it in more depth. Two of these teachers are now taking classes. Both of them, independent of each other, came to me to say thank you for all that they learned in our professional learning sessions. They both said that most of what they hear in class they have already learned at school. They also said that they are ahead of their peers because of the work we have done with literacy and that their classmates look to them for support. An unsolicited evaluation such as this is tremendously validating and encouraging for a coach.

Any time a teacher asks for a literacy coach's opinion, asks the coach to visit his class, asks the coach to demonstrate a lesson, or asks the coach to listen to a child read, the coach is getting feedback on the work she is doing. I encourage you to let these pieces of informal, evaluative information pile up in your head. Literally give yourself a mental image of something that accumulates: old newspapers or undelivered mail at the post office. If we took all these pieces of positive information that we receive and let them pile up, if we recognized the magnitude of the work we and the teachers with whom we work are doing, and if we understood that we can intelligently and systematically take care of ourselves, then we would be able to do our jobs even better.

Focusing on our positive feedback—solicited or unsolicited—isn't always easy, and we tend to let the negative feedback pile up in our minds and send the positive feedback out with the morning trash. For example, for the first three years I was out of undergraduate school, I taught the same group of students at each subsequent grade level. Among that group was a child—we'll call her Jane—who struggled terribly. I honestly had little idea of how to help her. I had been taught that if I just surrounded children with books they would learn to read from sheer exposure. In my undergraduate work I received little, if any, specific information about how to help children learn to read. In college I learned of some lovely children's books, and I made a game to reinforce vowel sounds, but this did little to equip me for the real world of literacy instruction.

Jane's parents grew angry with me, and I couldn't blame them. I was never able to help Jane, and the dismay associated with that effort was what pushed me toward graduate work in literacy. Toward the end of our third year together, her father wrote me a horrible note. He was furious, and the contents of the letter were unkind and even inappropriate. However, on some level, I felt that his harsh words were justified. To some extent they assuaged my guilt.

One night years later, during the time when I was working on my doctorate, I was out with some other teaching assistants. Something triggered my memory of Jane, and I told my friends the whole story. Then, to their amazement, I pulled the letter out of my purse and read it to them. They were taken aback, not by the father's harshness, but by the fact that I carried this horrible note with me everywhere I went.

My friends made me ceremonially light the letter on fire in the candle at our table! This felt good, not so much because I was getting rid of the note, but because my friends had given me permission to let go of my sense of hurt and failure, and they had validated me enough to help me move forward. To my surprise, each of them had taught a "Jane" and received a similar note. It is difficult in our most dejected states to recognize the universality of most human experiences. Unlike me, however, my friends had shed their guilt years prior or at least had figured out how to put their culpability in "Jane's" situation into a place that was safe for them.

I have received many kind notes from parents, but these never make it into my purse for long-term reflection. It is much easier for us to hang on to our failures than our successes, and we hold onto our really big failures very tightly. This is a habit most of us have developed; perhaps guilt is the currency with which we buy our way into our success driven culture.

I am a different person now. I keep positive relics stashed all over my life. I am strategic in psychologically setting the hurtful messages ablaze in my head, and I try to linger over gestures that are emotionally reinforcing. I'm not always successful. There are too many people in my school and in my life for everyone to be constantly satisfied with me, so I receive my share of negative messages. However, I usually get enough positive responses to keep my psyche afloat, and I am learning to tread water for myself a little bit, too.

Coaches should literally collect positive souvenirs of their work life. There are encouraging artifacts that stamp our lives, and we need to save them and let them accumulate. Anytime someone tells us in writing something positive about our work, we should hold on to it. As we coach, literacy instruction and, consequently, literacy learning begin to change for the better in our schools. People send us e-mails or handwritten notes thanking us for our work or noticing when we have done something well. Perhaps if we literally collect bits of positivity and file them, our minds will develop the habit of looking for the positive in the work we do.

I print out every positive or encouraging e-mail I receive and keep a hard copy, along with any handwritten notes, in a file. When I get discouraged—and sometimes I get really discouraged—I can pull out this file and read from it. These artifacts are a lifeboat when I become overwhelmed or frightened by the high seas of change. They help me pull away from the undertow of despair that occasionally grabs me, or they simply reinforce my sense of safety. It is comforting at the sight of an approaching storm to know there is a raft of hope to reach for when we need it.

Souvenirs

In navigating educational change, data become our map to student achievement. It is critical that we know our data and that we act on them, rather than spending excessive time in data collection and analysis or acting without looking thoughtfully at data at all. Data brings with them challenges, and we have to be prepared to make room for the necessary discomfort they may impose on teachers while also offering them hope, a vision, and extensive support. Furthermore, evaluation should influence every corner of our work, including the places where we look honestly at ourselves.

The Reasons:
Coaching Matters

CHAPTER 9

Educating Everyone: Looking at Difference Differently and at Ourselves Honestly

"[W]hy open your mouth if not to shout?"
Stephen Dobyns, "The Ionius Monk," *Common Carnage*, 1996, p. 78

You have had 8 chapters to get to know me. You know about my twins, my baby, and my personal interests. You also know my voice as a writer and, when I haven't explicitly told you, you have probably been able to infer my philosophy of life or how I interpret the world around me. So let's try a little experiment.

I want you to imagine my family. We are a middle-income family of five. I am a petite 39-year-old with relatively short hair and brown eyes. My fraternal twins, Christopher and Duncan, are thin and tall; Christopher wears glasses. The twins look enough alike that people often speak of them emphatically, "Well, they're definitely identical twins." My youngest son, Natie, which is short for Nathaniel, is 4, and he has long, dark, curly hair that has never been cut. Most people think he is a girl, and he has learned to say, "I'm a boy," and "That's OK." My husband, Nate, is long-legged and thin with black hair. He is a photographer and always wears a camera in a case attached to his belt. He wears long-sleeved dress shirts and long pants every day of the year, except when he plays tennis.

Can you see us in your mind's eye? We are a typical American family. How do you imagine us? Are we standing in a row? Are we on our front porch? Are we holding hands? Am I White or Black? Is my husband White or Black? Why do you think you imagined us as you did?

I write to you as a bird enthusiast, a pianist, a gardener, a mother, and a White woman married to a Black man. Certainly the ideas presented in this chapter are dear to me; they have become less abstract and more personal. I live in this overlapping space between two races, and it affords me some interesting and difficult insights. Ideas are constantly shifting in my head as I work to move my mind and my heart beyond the racial identity I have developed during my largely segregated, middle class life.

Eighty-three percent of teachers are White (Strizek, Pittsonberger, Riordan, Lyter, & Orlofsky, 2006, p. 3), and most were trained by White professors at colleges with a predominantly White student population (Snyder, Tan, & Hoffman, 2006, p. 278). Although students of color are not evenly divided among schools, they make up 40% of the students in public education (Strizek et al., p. 4). I do not know of any data on the racial makeup of literacy coaches. However, literacy coaches come from a predominantly White pool of teachers. This means that, for the most part, White literacy coaches are coaching White teachers on how to teach students of color.

Juxtapose this against the tremendous academic achievement gap between Black and White students, and one is likely to wonder if the two are somehow connected. Irvine addresses the racial differences between students and teachers, stating, "most of the teachers who instruct these failing culturally diverse students do not share their students' ethnic backgrounds" (2003, p. xviii).

The Purposes of This Chapter

As a coach I am in a position of leadership and, as such, people look to me for my opinions. What I say as well as what I do in regard to teaching students of color has the potential to affect my school culture at-large as well as the individual teachers with whom I work, not to mention the lives of the hundreds, even thousands, of children they will teach.

This chapter contends that I, as a White person and a literacy coach, need to initiate and engage in conversations about the role of race in our schools and that I need to begin to recognize the corresponding privileges that continue to reinforce and perpetuate subtle but dangerous and systemic forms of racism in United States society. Educator and activist bell hooks (1995) encourages me, as a "righteous white" person (p.188), to explore the way my position in society influences how I read the world because, even though I have never been a hatemonger, I am still a member of the racial group with the most power, which gives me influence for good or bad. hooks enlists White people along with Black people to "construct models for social change" (p. 193). As a White person in general and a literacy coach in particular, I play a part in this construction.

My efforts in the next few pages are three-dimensional. On one level, this is simply a story I need to tell. On another level, I want to illustrate how one person is learning to look honestly at her own prejudices and at the privileges that systemic racism affords her. Most important, however, I want the students of color in my school to improve their academic achievement, and I want all of the teachers and students in our school to understand the relation among literacy, activism, and change.

This chapter tells my story of racial-identity development. Because I am White and this story is autobiographical, it may speak more loudly to White readers. However, the story is also about self-reflection, honesty, justice, action, and love. On those counts at least, I hope that people of all ethnicities find something in this chapter to which they can connect.

I realize that prejudice and racism are not easy subjects to broach. My hope is that by now you trust me a little bit and that you have grown at least somewhat comfortable with my voice. At the very least, maybe you know that if I talk about something this delicate and this personal, I do so with respect for you, whatever your perspectives.

Defining Terms

As mentioned before, multiculturalism and racial identity are not my fields of expertise. I have rewritten this chapter from scratch four different times over two years, based on feedback I have received from colleagues and reviewers who work in the field. When academics read this chapter, they tend to want my content and voice to be more scholarly. When coaches and teachers read this chapter, they tend to appreciate its accessibility.

I have learned what should have been obvious—that scholarliness and accessibility run at cross-purposes. I have found myself caught in a perpetual loop of revision as I have tried to consider competing audiences. In the end, however, I am writing this for literacy coaches, so I have chosen to keep the voice straightforward and I tend to make generalizations based on personal experience. I hope that this chapter will stand up to some academic scrutiny; however, I have decided that audiences of literacy coaches and audiences of university professors will read this chapter with different expectations, and if I need to bend, it will be in the direction of literacy coaches.

Favoring coaches as an audience for this chapter does not relieve me of an obligation to get my information straight. For purposes of clarity, I offer somewhat academic definitions of the terms I use throughout this chapter. In order to communicate about issues of race and privilege I must categorize people and label ideas, but all this categorizing and labeling is flawed. For example, White people are also people of color, capitalizing the first letter in racial identities may give them too much importance, racial categories aren't mutually exclusive, and the term *racism* is likely to make some people close this book. Nevertheless, the following definitions represent my efforts toward clarity, despite their limitations.

I have chosen to use the definitions of terms that Tatum uses in her book *"Why Are All the Black Kids Sitting Together in the Cafeteria?" and Other Conversations About Race* (1997). Although her book is almost 10 years old now, her definitions are clear and straightforward, and her book has been a pivotal one for me.

I know that my growth is faster when I can focus less on terminology and more on ideas and conversations. Tatum writes, "It is difficult to talk about what is essentially a flawed and problematic social construct without using language that is itself problematic" (p. 17). It is my hope that you can focus on the processes presented here rather than on the awkward way I describe them.

First, I use the term *White* to refer to Americans of European descent and the term *people of color* to refer to people of African descent, people of Asian descent, people of Latin American descent, and indigenous people. I use *Black* rather than *African American* because I feel it is more accurate; there are a lot of Black people who are not from Africa.

Furthermore, I capitalize both *Black* and *White* because one's racial identity is important in American society and because typically most racial identifications are capitalized (e.g., Asian, African, European,

Hispanic). I do not use the word *minorities* because it is misleading; "minorities" presently represent the majority of the world (Tatum, p. 15).

The two terms that are particularly emotionally charged in this chapter are *prejudice* and *racism*. I have learned that these terms are not interchangeable, as I once thought. *Prejudice* refers to our individual— often misinformed—predetermined views of people and groups. People usually learn prejudice without realizing it; prejudice is taught as the subtext to our societal mechanisms. *Prejudice* refers to individuals and their actions, as opposed to the actions of society at-large.

Racism, on the other hand, moves beyond the individual and prejudice. Tatum writes that racism "is not only a personal ideology based on racial prejudice, but a *system* involving cultural messages and institutional policies and practices..." (p. 7). For example, if my picture is on the back of a book and if, because of stereotypes of Black intellectual inferiority, someone selects it over a book with a Black author on the back, I am unknowingly benefiting from my whiteness and the racism in our society, even though I would not be comfortable with such a decision if I knew of it.

Finally, *racial-identity development*, which is what this story is largely about, refers to the individual process of figuring out what it means to belong to a particular racial group. So generally speaking, the story that follows is primarily about me figuring out what it means (from my perspective) to be White and how my whiteness fits into the larger context of society in the United States and my work as a literacy coach.

My Story

The first person I knew who was of a different ethnicity than I was the housekeeper we had when I was 5. Her name was Bernice, and she was Black. One day I was riding in the car with my mother and passed an elementary school of Black children. The school had just been dismissed, and my mother stopped at the crosswalk as the children crossed the street. I had never seen any Black people besides Bernice; I thought she was the only one. I said, "Mama, look at all of Bernice's children!"

Presently, my understandings and investigations of ethnicity and racial identity are a bit more complex. However, my perspectives are still limited. I would never have thought that someone could be married to a person of a different race and continue to feel prejudice toward his race. My husband and I have each other to speak to honestly about assumptions, events, and misconceptions that are shaped by our different cultural experiences, and these conversations are always enlightening. I certainly never thought that my prejudices (the ones I never even recognized having in the first place) affected how I dealt with children. Basically, I never thought about racial inequities and how I perpetuate them. I have just lived according to the same myths that have influenced all of the other White middle class people I know.

I grew up certain that I was not prejudiced and grew into someone who is certain that she is. I never participated knowingly in any racist acts, but I grew up in a culture where people were not uncomfortable accentuating their perceptions of racial superiority. These perceptions manifested themselves in racial jokes, disrespectful and unkind behaviors toward people who were different, and a pervasive sense of better-than-ness.

I am afraid that my racial-identity development is probably pretty typical for a White middle class person, and statistically it is probably pretty typical for most teachers. Unfortunately, my learned biases have most likely seriously influenced how I have interacted with children of color and, worse, I haven't even known it. The myths that follow describe assumptions common among White middle class people; I grew up believing these myths were reality.

Racism for me has always been defined by acts of violence and hatred "perpetuated by horrible others" (Applebaum, 2003, p. 9). Overt forms of racism were not demonstrated or endorsed by my family, but from the larger environment in which I existed, I learned the lessons below. Because this chapter is autobiographical, most of the stories I include deal with assumptions White or middle class people often make about Black or poor people; however, I do try to make some connections to other types of differences. Again, my hope is that you can see the process behind the labels.

Myth #1: People who don't have as much as I do, have what they deserve. Given that my society is founded on the idea of the American Dream and the equality of humankind, anyone can "make it" in the United States. So if someone hasn't made it, it is because of something she did or didn't do. Poverty is a consequence of poor choices, laziness, or even sin. "These people" are, whether by twist of fate or act of God, where they are because they deserve to be; poverty is what they have earned.

Middle class conversations about race or poverty inevitably begin and end with examples of people who are poor, and often of color, who have been successful, thus substantiating the myth that our society is a meritocracy and all people need do to succeed is apply themselves. The thinking among the people I know is that the farther "up" a person has come, the stronger the case that hard work is the great equalizer. Thus, any success is earned, as is any failure. Furthermore, any advantage, because it is earned, is also deserved. This of course means that my family is deserving, and people in poverty (often people of color) are there for fair reasons that have nothing to do with me.

Myth #2: Because I am White, I am better than others who are not, and my customs, beliefs, and opinions are the "right" ones. And because people with little material wealth deserve what they have, they must not be very good people. Our society has clearly communicated this to all racial groups and all socioeconomic levels. Of course, few people would come right out and admit they think that White people are better than people of color, but most White people are taught this at an early age. A young White woman in a teacher preparation program examined her cultural biases and was shocked to learn that she had racist beliefs she had never recognized. Allen (in press) writes of the woman's early perceptions of racial superiority: "Again, no one told me I was better, I saw it. The white children had better grades. The white mothers volunteered at the school. The teachers were white. The principal was white. And the lunch ladies were black..." (p. 51).

The facts of this story are straightforward to me; identifying grades and labeling jobs are objective exercises. My challenge is in naming the more insidious message: People who make better grades are better people, and people who have better jobs (i.e., jobs that make more money) are also better people. hooks (1994) speaks to our stereotypes of the poor:

> Contemporary popular culture in the United States rarely represents the poor in ways that display integrity and dignity. Instead, the poor are portrayed through negative stereotypes. When they are lazy and dishonest, they are consumed with longing to be rich, a longing so intense that it renders them dysfunctional. Willing to commit all manner of dehumanizing and brutal acts in the name of material gain, the poor are portrayed as seeing themselves as always and only worthless. (p. 168)

I have always believed in the inverse relationship between poverty and integrity. When we were first married, my husband owned a small house that we decided to keep as a rental property after he moved out. This house would probably be affordable for some families of limited financial resources. When we were first considering renting it, we talked to many people about how to go about finding "good" tenants.

I suggested instead that we sell the house. I felt that renting in that income bracket was likely to bring headaches. Without realizing it, I was inadvertently letting my prejudice show. I was saying that we shouldn't rent to poor people and, because that house was only likely to attract poor people, we should just sell the house. My husband told me emphatically (and I still remember the exact moment I understood this idea) that there were plenty of honest, hard-working, dependable poor people and that we just needed to find them. I responded, "Really?"

A few years ago I participated in a workshop for educators entitled "A Framework for Understanding Poverty" by Ruby Payne, a former teacher and administrator, and president of a publishing company dedicated to helping educators better understand how to teach children from poverty. There is a lot of controversy around her work, and my point is not to criticize or endorse her. Payne married someone who grew up in poverty and this gave her a different perspective on people who live in poverty. I remember she said something like "I didn't understand until I married someone in poverty." My immediate thought was, "Why would she marry someone in poverty?" My prejudices were that strong!

Myth #3: Poor people or people of races and cultures different from mine do not love their children as much as I love mine. I have always thought that people who love their children demonstrate affection in the ways middle class parents do. Loving parents read to their children. They show that they care about their children's education by being room mothers and attending PTA meetings. They give them things such as nice clothes, a car, and a private education. They spend money on them.

Throughout my life, my parents have demonstrated affection toward me in a number of different ways. Often it has been shown through gifts. This is one of the ways I have known that they love, approve of, and appreciate me. This has led me to unwittingly wonder how people without the resources to buy things for their children can truly love them. How do these parents effectively express affection for their children?

How do the children know they are loved? Aren't the feelings of love that are displayed in grandiose ways deeper than feelings of love expressed simply? These ideas seem gross and illogical to me now. Unfortunately, they are still prominent in our schools.

In *Con Respecto: Bridging the Distances Between Culturally Diverse Families and Schools: An Ethnographic Portrait*, Valdés (1996) writes of Saúl, whose parents were Mexican-origin immigrants and the assumptions his teacher, Mrs. Lockley, made of his mother, Velma.

> For Mrs. Lockley, part of Saúl's problem was the "fact" that the parents were not "involved" in his education. She pointed to her lack of communication with Velma as evidence of both disinterest and lack of involvement. She had sent notes home with Saúl that were never responded to. Velma would simply not come to school to talk to her. (p. 4)

Valdés goes on to write that Velma

> did not, however become more "involved" at school in ways in which the teacher could see or understand. It was thus easy for Mrs. Lockley and the other teachers to conclude that the Soto family, like so many Mexican families, simply did not "care" about their children's education. (p. 5)

The idea that parents who are poor or who are of color do not love their children as much as White, middle class parents love their children is still one of the bedrock beliefs in many schools, whether it is spoken aloud or not.

Ritchie (2006) interviewed preservice teachers, exploring their beliefs about working with children of different cultures. He quotes Stephanie, a master's degree student in a large southeastern research university.

> Um, I think that's a difference in our culture; I think education is much more important...to the White culture than it is to the African American culture. Um, and I think that's sad, but at the same time it's, it's their way of culture and if it's not important to them, either that's going to have to be changed, or we have to work with the individual kids. We can't change the whole culture.... (p. 14)

Whether I think the racism in the paragraph example is overt or subtle, it is unfortunately not unusual. Statements such as, "Our parents can't even write their own names, so they sure don't know how to take care of their children," "He needs someone at home to speak English to him," "She's doing well considering her home situation," "I can't even get her mother to come in and talk with me," and "I wish I could just take her home with me" reveal the insidious prejudices that we must ferret out if we want to effectively teach children of color. What is most disturbing is that I have thought or said most of these things myself.

Despite society's continued efforts to convince me otherwise, I am learning that the vast majority of parents of every race and socioeconomic group love their children. I am beginning to recognize and understand that there are many ways for parents to show love to their children. hooks (2001) writes a lot about love and its place in schools and society:

> Even though a huge majority of destitute, poor, and working class black folks may find it more difficult than their more privileged counterparts to create loving environments, material privilege does not ensure that one will be raised in a loving home. Loving black families exist cross-class. (p. 47)

Myth #4: Racism doesn't really exist anymore. "Slavery is over" is a common statement of White people who are frustrated by racial-equity efforts. I think it is safe to say that most people in the United States, regardless of race or socioeconomic level, have heard this sentiment. However, most people who are Black, Hispanic, Jewish, Arabic, or any ethnicity other than White, understand that racism is not over in the United States. Unfortunately some of us, including myself, are just beginning to truly understand this.

Most White people see a racist as something or someone obvious like a "hood-wearing Klan member" or an "Archie Bunker figure" (Tatum, 1997, p. 11). However, we perpetuate racism when we don't speak up when someone tells a racist joke; when we don't push for the library to carry books written by people of color; or when we inadvertently support exclusionary practices in college admissions, hiring practices, or housing policies. We support racism when we accept the wide achievement gaps between rich and poor, Black and White, and native English speakers and English-language learners.

When someone says, "Slavery is over," she implies that there are now equal opportunities for Black people. However, the statement should more accurately imply that people of color, homosexuals, people in poverty, women, and other subordinate groups are now more likely to get equal opportunities than they have been previously. Things are better now for a lot of people; however, this doesn't necessarily mean that things are good.

Unpacking the Myths

How could I have held such strong biases and not let them come to bear on my work with children? How might such assumptions affect the work of teachers of children of color and of poverty? Can the implied belief that the parents of poor children are lazy translate into less communication with the parents and lowered expectations of students? Honestly, in what ways do we as educators and the education system communicate condescension to parents? How good are we at assuming goodwill of parents? How can I as a literacy coach combat such myths and misunderstandings within myself and among teachers?

The Cost of Privilege

Recognizing my privilege has been another difficult step in this long flight of stairs I am climbing. I am learning that the influence of the privilege associated with being a part of the dominant culture is tremendous, and it hurts me to recognize just how much it affects my life because, by definition, if I am receiving more, then someone else is receiving less. Privilege presently makes my life easier—will defining and exploring it make it harder?

Perhaps. But while recognizing and acknowledging the privileges I receive has been difficult and painful, it has already made my life better. My unacknowledged prejudice and the systemic racism to which it contributed were hurting me, even though I didn't see many symptoms. Furthermore, it gives me deep joy to be able to face this challenge and break the cycle of misunderstanding that my children have already begun to internalize.

McIntosh's (1990) article, "White Privilege: Unpacking the Invisible Knapsack," lists a few of the privileges that come with being White. For example, I can find housing without difficulty; when schools study our national heritage, my race is widely represented; and when I need an adhesive bandage, I can easily find one that matches my skin. McIntosh's article has been a great resource for me to explore how privilege serves me. However, recognizing my privilege as an individual is only a first step in understanding privilege. Unfortunately, the critical issue is not the privilege or the prejudice of one person, but the collective privilege that is built on institutional structures supported by the collective prejudice of racism. McIntosh writes, "Disapproving of the systems won't be enough to change them.... Individual acts can palliate, but cannot end, these problems" (p. 8).

When I go into a bookstore I generally do not think at all about my race or income level. However, the fact that I have a college education, the fact that I have been exposed to a wide range of topics, and the fact that I enjoy reading all grew out of the soil of privilege in which my life was planted. In this same bookstore I don't have to wonder if the inattentive service I receive is because of the prejudicial feelings of the bookstore employees. Most of the books in the store are written by members of my race. I don't have to make sure that my gestures are large and that I am open and obvious when I handle any material so that I won't be accused of stealing something. The clerk won't talk down to me because of my skin color or my dialect. Maybe I won't have to present identification when I use my credit card. Most of the people in the store will look, act, and talk like me.

The fact that I am White and socioeconomically advantaged never occurs to me the entire time I am in the bookstore, even though both have benefited me throughout my shopping experience. I cannot separate myself from the privilege associated with my membership in the dominant race, although most of my life I have been oblivious to the benefits it has afforded me. "Those with power are frequently least aware of—or least willing to acknowledge—its existence. Those with less power are often most aware of its existence" (Delpit, 1995, p. 24).

Deciding to Change

In the following section, I describe for you the stages I have worked through in an effort to understand and accept my whiteness and the privilege I enjoy because of large-scale, institutionalized racism. This is my process; I do not write of these stages as standardized phases in developing racial identity. While I present these stories as my own, from what I have read and from conversations with other White people exploring their racial identity, it does seem that some of the issues I have worked through have been documented as "normal" events in the development of a rational "White identity." So, where applicable, I have included some of the related quotes, research, and anecdotes I have found in the literature. However, I make no claim that this is an exhaustive literature review, as that is not my intent. I do hope that my story will challenge the racial assumptions of other literacy coaches and prompt them to explore their own racial identities and support teachers as they do the same.

For me, the whole process of examining and potentially changing my racial and cultural beliefs required a catalyst. I didn't just get up one morning and say to myself, "You know, I think I'm much more racist than I have realized." Marrying a person of a different race gave me a startling perspective on racism and a frightening mirror in which to look. "Waking up" required learning that I was not already awake, and I had to experience a pinch for that to happen.

The Stages of Grief

In retrospect, the stages of racial-identity development through which I have worked and am still working have resembled the classic stages of grief described by Kübler-Ross (1969). I have worked through "denial," "anger," "depression," and "acceptance" and have replaced "bargaining" with "action," which has occurred for me later in the process. For me there were two losses that prompted grief. First, I experienced the loss of myself as an individual. Recognizing my whiteness situated me as a member of a racial group and eliminated my option of separating myself from the egregious actions of others of my race. Most White people I know don't think of themselves as members of a racial group. They just think of themselves as "normal."

Second, I experienced the loss of the person I thought I was. This has been devastating for me. These new understandings and my wakefulness within them marked the death of the nonprejudiced me I have always thought was authentic. Both of these losses were significant for me, and the emotions through which I have struggled in my efforts to understand them have been predictable.

My movement through these stages has not, however, been linear. I can be in different stages, with different experiences or ideas, all at the same time. I can act by writing about racism tonight, and tomorrow I can have a thought or say something about which I will later feel guilty and perhaps resume denying my place of benefit. I can see an image or hear something on the radio that makes me angry. My son can say something negative about the "brown-skinned" children at school, and it will make me sad. But as I have habituated this process of reflection and exploration, I am spending less time feeling guilty, angry, or sad and more time taking action.

Stage 1: Denial. Denial can grow from at least two places, both of which are applicable to this conversation. I am likely to deny things when they are just too horrible for me to accept. I may also deny something because I feel guilty or because the admission will expose me as "bad." From my experience, and from what I have read, it appears that denial within this work often stems from the latter, a sense of guilt.

In the literature I have read in preparation for writing this chapter, there is much talk about the "White guilt" that accompanies change, and this guilt is something with which I have grappled. Iyer, Leach, and Pedersen (2004) have defined guilt as "an extremely unpleasant feeling based in a self-focused sense of responsibility for immorality" (p. 351). Unfortunately, this guilt is part of the "wear and tear" of racism. Although I have learned that guilt can eventually give way to other emotions, which eventually lead to action, I have also learned that it is largely unavoidable for White people who are trying to understand privilege and racism. Titone (1998) writes,

> In the context of teaching prospective and in-service teachers about culture and education, I have learned to expect that white people who first come face to face with the concepts of racism and their own complicity in maintaining a system from which they benefit, will feel not only very uncomfortable but also deeply wounded in the process of exploring it. (p. 167)

There is pain tied to this reflection and honesty because if I, with even the best of intentions, have actually been perpetuating stereotypes that reinforce prejudices I did not even believe I had, then I have unwittingly engaged in behaviors that were not in the best interest of the children and teachers with whom I have taught and worked. I can't scrutinize my thinking under this magnifying glass of honesty and not feel remorse.

Denial can manifest in at least a couple of forms. I might try to argue the uncomfortable information away, or I might simply turn away from it, choosing instead to ignore it altogether. I was not surprised to see that in the literature on racial-identity development, many people choose not to face the discomfort associated with this work. I know that I have done this before. Tatum (1997) writes, "Responses to this discomfort may include denying the validity of the information that is being presented, or psychologically or physically withdrawing from it" (p. 98).

On the other hand, the potential benefits of "sticking out" this uncomfortable process are tremendous. "If the individual remains engaged, he or she can turn the discomfort into action" (Tatum, p. 99). It is possible that "progressive white people" who oppose racism can recognize and understand the ways in which our cultural practices strengthen White privilege, while they are also negotiating and/or avoiding potentially paralyzing guilt or denial (hooks, 2001, p. 177).

Eventually I had to let go of my guilt for the most part because, while a necessary stage in processing my new understandings, it was turned inward and I knew that it was not a healthy emotional place for me to linger. Letting go of guilt continues to be particularly difficult because I am now awake to my continued inaccurate, unfair, and unkind sentiments toward people who are different from me. Unfortunately, being alert to my prejudices hasn't stopped me from having them.

Stage 2: Anger. Once I recognized my prejudices and began to work past my denial and my guilt, I developed some deep anger. During reading in preparation to write about this, I learned of many different types of anger that can be a part of a person's efforts to understand racism; I have felt many of these. I felt angry toward my parents for supporting my development of prejudicial thought, even though they, no more than I, saw or understood it. I also felt angry toward White people in general for making me look and feel like a bad person. Tatum (1997) writes of a White person struggling through developing a White identity. She quotes, "I am starting to feel angry toward my race for ever using this advantage toward personal gains" (p. 102).

From what I read, it appears that some people even get angry toward people of color and have to work through feelings that it is all their fault. I didn't experience this type of anger, but I can certainly understand how someone might go through a period of feeling this way. Tatum also quotes this person as saying, "I resent the minority groups. I mean, it's not my fault that society has deemed us 'superior'" (p. 102).

Stage 3: Depression. My process of developing racial identity, which is still in progress, has left me heavy with sadness at times. The challenges sometimes make me cry. The reading associated with this work has been exceedingly distressing. Issues of racism weigh heavy on me and, in studying extensively about them, I can easily find myself mired in a deep sense of hopelessness.

I have been wrestling with these feelings of despair around personal and societal ills off and on for a few years now, but I am beginning to wrestle less and think and act more. The discomfort associated with owning a piece of current racial inequities is a necessary part of my growth, and it is OK for me to be sad. I just have to redirect my energies at some point. Otherwise, I risk shutting down.

On the other hand, there have been times when I have felt strong within this work, and I have wanted to face the hard issues. I have at times immersed myself in the most candid information, watching videos, reading books, and engaging in conversations. In short, sometimes I just need to be sad, and I need for this sadness to be OK. It's like watching a movie and having a good cry. The tension builds within me, and sometimes I need to just let it accumulate until it reaches an emotional climax and then I emerge from it stronger and wiser.

Stage 4: Acceptance. In previous chapters we have talked at length about resistance to change and the avoidance behaviors that are sometimes indicative of this hesitancy. But resistance, denial, avoidance, and grief have reached a pinnacle for me around my misunderstandings about prejudice and racism, because I really want to be a "good" person.

However, I have come to understand that admitting prejudice and acknowledging racism does not make me an evil person; it makes me an honest person. Exposure to the judgments of others (family, friends, colleagues), or even judgments from myself, has been the main obstacle to looking honestly at my own prejudicial feelings and behaviors and how they are nestled in societal racism. I didn't want anyone to think of me as bad person. Marx and Pennington (2003) write, "all of our students/participants tended to associate goodness with nonracist identities. Thus, naming racism within themselves was at first cause for great alarm" (p. 105).

hooks (1994) describes, however, the healing role that loving ourselves and others can play in this process:

If we discover in ourselves self-hatred, low self-esteem, or internalized white supremacist thinking and we face it, we can begin to heal. Acknowledging the truth of our reality, both individual and collective, is a necessary stage for personal and political growth. This is usually the most painful stage in the process of learning to love—the one many of us seek to avoid. Again, once we choose love, we instinctively possess the inner resources to confront the pain. Moving through the pain to the other side we find the joy, the freedom of spirit that a love ethic brings. (p. 248)

Titone (1998) speaks to this need to heal that I have experienced. She suggests that we must help ourselves heal by reading, thinking, and talking with trusted others. These efforts can help us move beyond denial, guilt, and hopelessness. "It is more than intellectual work; it is work of the spirit" (pp. 167–168). Taking care of myself in this way has helped me heal enough to move my attention from myself and onto the problem.

Step 5: Action. Effectively raising consciousness about racism must also point the way toward constructive action. Constructive action can take many forms, and I have found great comfort in knowing that there are meaningful efforts I can make toward resisting racism and perpetuating a better society for myself and for my family.

First, one of the most valuable actions I have taken is seeking the support of others, White and Black, who are or have been working through their own racial identity. I need antiracist "allies" in my daily life. While studying racism has been angering and saddening at times, talking with someone who understands my struggle and who is farther along this continuum of growth and has been a real source of hope for me. Hope is empowering and has given me the strength to take action, such as writing this chapter.

Second, I can appreciate the power of baby steps. Although systemic attacks on racism that come from many directions are desperately needed, I know that I do not have to commit to great gestures to act. "Micro-level changes, such as those that take place within classrooms, are important, too" (Gay, 2000, p. 202). And once I understood that my role is not to "help the victims of racism, but to speak up against systems of oppression and to challenge other Whites to do the same" (Tatum, 1997, p. 109), I had a focus.

On an individual level, I can challenge racist comments. I really struggle with this, because I want these challenges to be within the context of kind assumptions and I don't want to make anyone feel like a "bad" person. More often than not, I figure out how to handle the situation long after it has passed. Then I am faced with the even bigger challenge of going back to the person and saying, "Do you remember what you said to me the other day about Hispanic children? Well..."

I can also begin to question those in authority about the policies and procedures I suspect are racist. I read of a White woman who told the library director in her town "that a sign in the children's room that read 'Unattended children will be sold as slaves' was offensive" (Lawrence & Tatum, 2004, p. 368). I know that I am strong enough to do something like this and that such efforts are valuable.

Third, I can begin to address institutional or systemic racism within and beyond my school. I can use my privilege to interrupt the cycle of racism in which my children have already engaged (Miner, 1995). Delpit speaks of a conversation with some young White women who were in teacher preparation programs. They were exceedingly uncomfortable with recognizing the power they possessed because of their privilege. She said to them, "Having power is not bad, it's what you do with that power" (1995, p. 142).

While it is not my fault that racism exists, it is my responsibility to take action against it. Tatum (1997) writes,

> we are not at fault for the stereotypes, distortions and omissions that shaped our thinking as we grew up. To say that it is not our fault does not relieve us of responsibility, however. We may not have polluted the air, but we need to take responsibility, along with others, for cleaning it up. (pp. 6–7)

Fourth, I can develop relationships with people who are different from me. Some people suggest that I strategically develop relationships with people who are positive representations of their culture (Gladwell, 2005). However, I'm not confident I can define positive representation without my biases betraying me. I am instead simply trying to be strategic about really getting to know all kinds of people.

Most people are positive representations of their race and culture in one respect or another. Where I choose to seek out the antithesis of the stereotype and how I choose to recognize this and which traits I look for can be dangerous, so I must be careful. Who is a positive representation of his race? Is it the man who demonstrates a strong work ethic while shining shoes or sweeping up the school at night? Is it the person who earns fame, acquires wealth, or demonstrates scholarship? Is it the woman who works nights at a fast-food restaurant so that she can write during the day? Or is it all of the above?

And how deeply can I see into someone if I never get close enough? And how well do I choose whom to get close to when I am using the same perceptions that have failed me because of my prejudices? This is hard, risky work. But I'm learning that the payoffs can be tremendous.

Finally, the most important action I have taken is to read and study. The limitations of space and my understandings prevent me from discussing the various lines of thought and research currently influencing efforts to help educators and others recognize their prejudice and the racism that benefits them. However, studying these ideas is part of what has kept me moving.

I was able to gain some momentum in this process when I began to explore deficit thinking, or our tendency to focus on the skills children lack rather than the skills they have, and I started to recognize it in myself and in others. In its place, I began to explore the concept of "funds of knowledge" (González, Moll, & Amanti, 2005; Moll, Amanti, Neff, & González, 1992) and worked to support teachers in developing "visions of success" rather than "rationales for failure" (Delpit, 1992, p. 246). I am studying multiculturalism so that I can support multicultural education in my school as something more than February bulletin boards of Martin Luther King, Jr. and separate curriculums that teachers "do" as a unit of study when there is time (Nieto, 1999).

Coaching as Political Action

Maybe you are wondering what all this has to do with literacy coaching. Well, developing a racial identity and working to overturn racism have less to do with literacy coaching specifically and more to do with being human. They are related to literacy coaching in the way that the chapters on listening, taking care of ourselves, honoring confidentiality, and appreciating our emotions are related. All of these things make me a better coach and point me toward being a better person. Furthermore, if I demand of myself strict justifications for all the chapters in this book, you would be left with a dry, sterile read. I have compromised my deepest purposes if, while teaching him to read, I have inadvertently taught a child that he is not as good as someone with lighter skin. Tragically, I think I have done this.

I have learned that everything I do as a literacy coach makes a statement about what I believe. In an article describing her work exploring prejudice with her students, Michalove (1999) writes, "My activism has been primarily through my teaching" (p. 21). I have come to understand that teaching others, whether children or teachers, is a political act and every action I take carries with it a subtext.

Edelsky (2003) writes,

> Even when I'm not talking about politics, I'll be talking about politics because when we're faced with politically mandated programs it's more obvious than ever that teaching, especially teaching literacy, is political. And if our theories shape our teaching and if teaching is political, then our theories are political. (p. 10)

So by a number of means, I can try to express my theories and opinions through positive action. I can work to establish a school culture where it is safe to explore these difficult understandings, and I can facilitate these explorations by working with a checklist for developing professional learning in a "multicultural society" (Banks, 2001). I can demonstrate respect and care that won't change despite where teachers are on the continuum of racial-identity development. I can step out in front and tell my autobiography of racism and hopefully give others the freedom to be honest. Pennington writes of her work with college students, "After a year of portraying myself as a teacher of children of color, full of love and advice and knowledge, I told them [the college students] my own story about my racism, and it changed everything" (Marx & Pennington, 2003, p. 97).

I know that I am not responsible for anyone else's change journey. However, I do have indirect access to many children whose lives probably have been and may continue to be adversely affected by racism's influence in the classroom, and I cannot dismiss this any more than I can dismiss this opportunity to tell you this story. So I will try to coach toward the balance between demonstrating respect and encouraging teachers to "seriously challenge their deeply held beliefs, attitudes, values, and knowledge claims" (Banks, 2001, p. 14).

I can comfort, encourage, and coach. I can be vigilant in remaining reflective about my impressions of racial and other differences among the teachers who are my students. I can love teachers at the earliest and the latest stages of change and accept who they are regardless of their ability to be reflective around these complex issues. Finally, I can be generous of spirit when I talk to myself about my own struggles, recognizing that I am not unique in my efforts to transform my habits of thought. Many others have worked through this process and struggled through these understandings, and it isn't easy for anyone.

I have included the following rather angry prose poem that I wrote in response to a conversation I had with a principal in a predominantly Black middle school. Her comments were blatantly racist in my opinion. I took what she said personally, and I was terribly hurt; still, I did not say anything to her at the time. My anger eventually subsided and I forgave myself for not saying something to her at the point of the exchange. I chose to include the poem because it represents, both in the poem itself and in the context in which it was written, many of the ideas I have explored in this chapter: systemic racism, individual prejudice, anger, guilt (mine, for not saying anything), reflection (hers, when I finally did say something), forgiveness (of self and others), and action (that of picking up a pen).

How to Talk Bad About Black People in Public

When we went to lunch on Wednesday you gave me advice you thought I would appreciate and so you told me that if I wanted to talk bad about black people in public I could just call them Canadians like I might say *We went to a movie last night and there were a bunch of Canadians talking through it*

and when I got home I was thinking about your advice and I wondered what you would do if there were Canadians around and you still wanted to talk bad about black people and I had this idea that you could call them Germans and you could say *I work with all these Germans who were only hired because they're German and they took good jobs away from more qualified Americans*

and then I wondered what you would do if there were Canadians and Germans around and you just had to talk bad about black people and so I thought you could call them Russians so you could say something like *A family of Russians moved into the house across the street and that really destroys property values so we are going to have to move*

but what if there were Canadians and Germans and Russians around and you still really needed to talk bad about black people so I thought you should probably call them Papua New Guineans and then you would be able to say *I saw a talk show on government programs of forced sterilization of Papua New Guineans and I don't see what is so wrong with it and Papua New Guineans don't have any business reproducing any way*

and I was still thinking and trying to help you solve your problem about needing to talk bad about black people in public and I thought about you calling them tree-huggers, cat lovers, holy rollers, people with goiters, vegetarians, veterinarians, flat-chested prostitutes, tired men in old suits, big-rig drivers, overweight bowlers, bald smokers, homosexual blondes, competition fisherwomen, career mechanics or rodeo clowns and I finally decided that it will just be too hard to come up with a code word for black people because there are so many of all different kinds of people and I wouldn't want you to embarrass yourself

but I was so relieved to have solved your problem about talking bad about black people that I made myself forget about you and then I kissed my little Canadian good night and slipped into bed next to my long, dark Papua New Guinean, thinking of you only long enough to wonder if you would be able to sleep as well as we. You with that large foot crammed suffocatingly into your mouth.

I later expressed to her how I felt about what she had said, and she was receptive and apologetic. I deeply respected her capacity for self-reflection around this encounter, and we were able to develop a trusting professional relationship and engage in other frank conversations about prejudice and racism. This and other similar experiences have encouraged me to allow much room for mistakes—mine and others'. I see my continued gross misunderstandings and poor word choices around these topics, despite my sincere efforts toward understanding and clarity, and I know that my mistakes are promising learning opportunities.

Souvenirs

The learning that has most influenced my work with teachers is the learning in which I have engaged about myself. To recognize, accept, and explore my deepest thoughts and opinions about the teachers and children with whom I work has been the most troubling and the most productive work I have done. It is harder to be honest with myself than with anyone else, but leadership in a school is a responsibility of the heart and soul, and I have to be the first one to take this risk so that I can honestly support teachers as they do the same. No acquisition of content knowledge can compare to the value of working through this process. In my opinion, the work I speak of in this chapter is the most important work I have done as a human being and as a literacy coach.

In his autobiography, *Lucky Man*, Michael J. Fox (2002) writes of a phone conversation with fellow Parkinson's sufferer, Muhammad Ali: "For some reason, I returned his call from the phone in my bathroom. In the mirror I could see my eyes welling up as he said, in his eloquent whisper, 'I'm sorry you have this, but with both of us in this fight, we're going to win now'" (p. 238). Although the situations are obviously completely different here, I hold a similar sentiment when it comes to literacy coaching. I am hopeful in the knowledge that some of you might also take on this risky, difficult, and important work and that you will love the teachers who take it on so that they can better love and educate the children in your school. I do not want to cling to "uncritical hope" (Nieto, 1999, p. xx), but educators are a force, and I do not underestimate our potential to effect societal change.

CHAPTER 10

The Emotions of Coaching: How Does It Feel to Be a Literacy Coach?

"Do the thing you believe in. Do the best you can in the place where you are and be kind."
Helen Nearing, "Twilight and Evening Star," *Loving and Leaving the Good Life*, 1992, p. 183

My 4-year-old son has a pair of rubber boots that are green with frog eyes. Rain reminds him of his "frog boots" and the promise of puddles when the downfall subsides. Natie's protective frog boots provide him the safety to take risks and to go about his work of studying the properties of water. I wish I had protective gear for every aspect of life my children wade into, because the work of risk and growth over a lifetime is immense.

A literacy coach's efforts to positively influence a school are also monumental undertakings. When we, who are very small, take on very large puddles of need, we must outfit ourselves in protective emotions. We must wear hope, faith, joy, and love like frog boots, purple slickers, and turtle umbrellas. Then when the inevitable rains come, we will avoid becoming completely soaked. A little bit of warmth goes a long way, and it may be all we need to keep from washing away with the water of the storm.

We and the teachers in our schools are relatively small in comparison to the enormity of the reform needed in education. We must shod ourselves in the protective emotions that will make our work safe and enable us to better care for each other. We need to care for our emotional rain gear as if a big storm is coming, because it probably is. Our professional lives may very well rest in our emotional fortitude in the face of rising waters. Not only that, but if we drown in our professional lives, our personal lives will also get a soaking. Ready your galoshes and your umbrellas, the tide will inevitably rise.

Emotional "Hooks": The Emotions of Memory and Learning

When educational leadership is misguided or insensitive, teachers in a school suffer from the leader's lack of emotional consideration. Hargreaves and Fullan (2000) write, "In the drive to standardize teaching—to define and demarcate it through graded benchmarks of knowledge and competence—it is easy to lose sight of teaching's emotional dimension, of the enthusiasm, passion, and dedication that make many teachers great" (p. 53).

Most memories have an emotional core, whether positive or negative. Even those that we don't think of as laced with emotion probably are, otherwise we wouldn't remember them. For example, about 15 years ago I visited some friends who had just had their third child. Mandy commented that another friend of ours, Alice, had been visiting and that the visit had been rather bothersome. Mandy explained that Alice, who didn't have children, had trouble seeing how she made Mandy's life more difficult during an already difficult time. Mandy said, "She tries to help but then she does things like putting the knives in the dishwasher pointing up."

Now, 15 years later, I do not put knives in the dishwasher without thinking of this conversation. I point the knives down into the dishwasher and think about Mandy and all the emotions of that visit. For 15 years I have been reliving that experience every time I load the dishwasher. It was just a line of speech that stayed with me and doesn't seem particularly loaded with emotion. However, the conversation actually had many emotional layers.

First, I wanted children at the time and was anticipating motherhood, and it occurred to me that, until Mandy spoke of it, I had never thought about which way to put the knives in the dishwasher. Then I wondered if there were other very important details that I might miss when I was a mother. What if I hadn't talked about this with Mandy? Would my children have put their eyes out when they tripped over the open door of the dishwasher? And what should one do in such a situation: leave the knife in or pull it out? These are horrible thoughts, which is probably partially why they have stayed with me for so long.

On another level, I thought about Alice who, in an effort to help, had loaded the dishwasher in such a way as to endanger the health of the very people for whom she was trying to demonstrate care. How would she feel if she knew? I felt horribly sad for her, partly because of her mistake and partly because of the way Mandy was talking about her. I felt guilty, as if I was gossiping about or making fun of a friend. Then I wondered if there were times when I, in trying to be helpful, had in fact made a situation worse. How would I know if my efforts at kindness left a wake of catastrophe? Would Mandy be relieved when I left? Would she reflect on the ways I had endangered her children?

By sharing this emotionally laden anecdote I mean to demonstrate that the memories that hang in the closets of our heads rest on hooks of emotion. This one line of speech about loading knives in a dishwasher carried with it the hope of motherhood, the fear of failure, the embarrassment of ignorance, the guilt of deception, the joy of new life, and the anxiety of change. There are similar emotional fragments that occur throughout our days because it is impossible to parse our lives into emotional and professional sections. We should instead use this emotion to our advantage as we interact with rich, round, dynamic personalities. These efforts to focus on people and their emotional responses can keep our motives sincere, our work authentic, and our story lines engaging.

Emotion is a powerful tool for making our relationships, our teaching, our learning, and our work meaningful. Meaningful relationships, teaching, learning, and work are building blocks of authentic reflection and growth. Johnston (2004) writes, "intellectual life is fundamentally social, and language has a special place in it. Because the intellectual life is social, it is also relational and emotional" (p. 2). To try to engage in literacy coaching work outside of our own and teachers' capacities to feel would be to work against our own purposes. However, this is a common strategy in education; the field of education and educational reform is historically devoid of emotion. Hargreaves and Fullan (1998) write,

Emotions are virtually absent from the literature and advocacy of educational change in areas like strategic planning, cognitive leadership, problem-solving, or standards-based reform. Even the idea of organizational learning which is on the very cutting edge of change theory is almost exclusively cerebral in its emphasis. Teachers need to take more care of their own emotions, colleagues (with members) need to take more care of each other.... (p. 55)

Encouraging teachers to be emotionally awake at school can be messy. Scott (2002) says, "Life is curly. Don't try to straighten it out" (p. 15). Emotions are curly, too. Once again, there is risk in this work. Nevertheless, attending to how teachers feel has the potential to affect your school culture and the experiences of children as much as any content. Content without heart will not call to anyone; breathe some life into the same content, and teachers will hear it calling their names.

Several years ago when I was working as a language arts consultant, I misunderstood the subject of a workshop I was hired to present. The teachers had requested a workshop on preparing students for standardized tests. I somehow thought that the workshop was on time management and study skills. This was a pretty gross misunderstanding, and I'm still not sure how it happened, but I didn't learn of my mistake until I was standing in front of the teachers sharing information.

So I tried to shift gears to their preferred topic, for which I had not prepared and about which I knew little. It was as bad as one could imagine. I thought teachers were going to get up and walk out, and I still had two hours left. Somehow I managed to get teachers talking about their successes in helping children prepare for and do well on standardized tests. Gradually the group became engaged in the conversations, which were far more valuable than anything I had to tell them on the subject.

This was one of my worst experiences as a consultant until, in an act of desperation, I gave teachers an opportunity to share their experiences around testing, and the related emotions came tumbling out. I didn't interrupt or redirect the conversation because I had nothing else with which to fill the time.

At the end of the session, I nervously distributed the required evaluation forms. To my amazement, the feedback I received from teachers was unanimously positive. Their responses were even stronger than those of the teachers in a workshop the day before, when I had expertly aligned the content to the needs of the group. What had, I believe, made the workshop valuable was the combination of emotion generated in support of our discussions and conversations about valuable strategies. Marrying the two saved the professional learning experience.

Emotionally investing in our work and in teachers involves putting ourselves in a vulnerable position. Often, however, this act makes it safe for others to do the same. Given their relevance to our lives in and beyond literacy coaching, I would like to look individually at the emotions I consider most critical to our work.

Harboring Hope

Hope is the positive that happens despite the deep puddles. It is most valuable in the rainiest locales and the places where people are most fatigued, failure is most documented, and progress is most stunted. It is easy to be hopeful when things are progressing positively. However, "Hope's real value is when the conditions are not hopeful" (Hargreaves & Fullan, 1998, p. 57). Many days of continuous beautiful weather will make anyone optimistic. But it is the thunder, lightening, and rising waters that can wash away any sense of hope.

When I first began working as a literacy coach, I had many days where hope escaped me, and I would become mired in fear. Peggy Terrell, the language arts consultant I mentioned earlier, was my comforter and gave me a place to safely doubt. In my early days, we sometimes had to dig for hope. We mined it in our work and when we found a promising vein, we worked it like our professional lives depended on it, and they did. We held celebrations close and let even little ones count. We looked for hope in unexpected places and found it in our smallest successes.

The choices a literacy coach makes in working within a school can perpetuate or squash hope. The observations I did and the ways I chose to communicate with teachers were an investment that paid dividends of hope. Literacy coaches can communicate a vision, recognize positive trends in data, and demonstrate confidence in teachers to help both the teachers and themselves to remain hopeful. In *Pedagogy of Hope*, Freire (1994) writes of how he struggled with depression:

> At bottom, in seeking for the deepest "why" of my pain, I was educating my hope. I never expected things just to "be that way." I worked on things, on

facts, on my will. I *invented* the concrete hope in which, one day, I would see myself delivered.... (p. 22)

Similarly, we coaches must learn the alchemy of changing a school culture from leaden failure into golden optimism. However, inventing hope is both magic and science, and discovery is a path marked by failed attempts and barriers.

One of the biggest barriers to hope is isolation. Is it a coincidence that the field in which we work can be at once one of the most hopeless and one of the most isolating? Leonard and Leonard (2003) studied the challenges associated with collaborating in schools. They write: "What is particularly noteworthy, however, is that the realization and maintenance of schools as so-called 'professional learning communities' seems to remain, in many instances, little more than an elusive aspiration" (p. 9). Teachers often remain "mired in traditional norms of teacher individuality and organizational isolationism" (p. 10). Anything we can do to build a bridge between classrooms will contribute to a natural sense of hope. Kohler, Crilley, Shearer, and Good (1997) studied math coaches who worked with teachers in nine procedural areas. They found that "areas not routinely discussed with a coach showed little or no refinement" and that refinements to classroom practice were "more likely to occur under conditions of collaboration than independence" (p. 248). I envision coaches on ladders wearing safety goggles and cutting holes in the walls between classrooms, creating doorways and portals that connect teachers to each other. This will get us in trouble with our districts' risk management teams, but we must find other, safer ways to connect teachers.

The idea of connecting teachers reminds me of strands of twinkling lights that are wired in a series. If one light is out, none of the lights work, and there is a lot of energy expended in working with each one in an effort to get them all lit again. I don't think our struggles are quite this extreme, but the sense that every last person in our school collectives is critical and is directly connected to others in the community is worth the effort of pursuing for the promise of hope it carries with it. hooks (2003) writes, "Forging a learning community that values wholeness over division, disassociation, splitting, the democratic educator works to create closeness" (p. 49).

The very act of literacy coaching appears to develop relationships, even "companionship" (Slater & Simmons, 2001, p. 69). Helping teachers connect to one another makes the work environment feel safe. Hope rests in safety, and when teachers are insecure, they don't have the time or emotional energy to develop hope. It is not surprising that teachers might lose sight of hope. They get one change in place and then the change changes. They are under a hierarchy of scrutiny that goes from the general public to administrators. They are often working without the materials or the staff development necessary to implement the very things that are required. Hargreaves and Fullan (1998) write,

> Education happens when hope exceeds expectation. Teaching is what makes the difference. Teachers everywhere work miracles without many of the resources or supports they really need. Without hope, teaching is nothing. It stops being a mission and becomes just another job. Too many of our teachers are starting to lose hope. We are in serious danger of undermining a fundamental truth of educational effectiveness—that the learning and emotional lives of students are profoundly dependent on the learning and emotional lives of teachers. (p. 87)

Teachers manage the sheer physical exhaustion, the guilt for the children they do not reach, the emotional multitasking required to attend to a whole classroom of individual demands, and the understanding that there are forces bearing on the life of students over which teachers have no power. If teachers feel threatened, intimidated, doubted, or discouraged, then their emotional resources will be expended in finding something to hold onto and they will let go of hope in an effort to grab something else.

Finding Faith

Many literacy coaches will say that their priority is the children, and, at first glance this would seem appropriate. However, if our vision goes over, through, or around teachers in an effort to reach children, we will inevitably make decisions that will actually make us *less* effective. This is the paradox of coaching. To help children become better at reading and writing, we have to take our focus *off* them and move it onto the teachers, and a shift like this requires great faith of a literacy coach.

Faith is perhaps the trait that will best support a literacy coach. We need faith as much as we need content knowledge, organizational skills, and the ability to understand relationships. Faith gives us the strength to move in the direction of our moral purpose, which would otherwise feel unreachable. Work without faith feels like wasted time, and it will take us dangerously close to the trap of just going through the motions.

Without faith the meaning of our lives is compromised, and we will begin to engage in repetitive procedures that are without heart. We might begin to talk about the teachers or the children and what they can't, don't, or won't do. We might begin to explain away our lack of vision because it is too risky to take a leap of faith when there is the possibility of landing hard. To actually expect teachers and ourselves to succeed involves looking at all the circumstances, all the statistics, all the negative stereotypes, and all the previous efforts that have failed, and then believing that success is still possible.

Even our measure of success, "Was it a positive experience?" requires a large measure of faith, particularly when the positive experience is a fragile counterpoint to sturdy concerns. For example, the idea that the children can work in easier material and make more progress taxes our faith. When we are teaching our very hardest and children are working at maximum mental energy levels, we feel as if we are doing our jobs well. "She's such a hard worker," an administrator might remark. It seems counterintuitive to slow down teachers and children. But engaging in higher quality work in easier contexts is often better and, although it flies in the face of the work ethic in the United States which encourages us to give our "all," easier will probably take you and your school farther, because children will enjoy reading more and teachers will enjoy teaching more. However, choosing to set up students and teachers for success rather than to study their failures involves an act of faith.

Faith comes into play in literacy coaching constantly. Even assuming goodwill of someone requires a leap of faith sometimes. To assume that someone is trying to adopt a practice, is committed to change, and is interested in our support can be difficult in the face of strong evidence to the contrary. Even when we know that someone is not trying, is not committed, and is not interested, we must exercise a faith-based assumption of goodwill. Faith itself is counterintuitive and by definition disagrees with the evidence.

We are lucky. We work with teachers, and they already have immeasurable faith. They are the ones who work miracles with the children that society has already decided will fail. Certainly faith is the badge of any successful teacher. Hargreaves and Fullan (1998) cite an experience with one teacher:

> Patricia Murphy teaches a group of special-education children. Such children, she says are often labeled "emotionally disturbed, difficult, violent and unteachable." Her experience is different. She gets "to share in the progress and achievements of a group of children who know the odds are against them, but learn anyway." In Patricia Murphy's eyes, teaching is inherently hopeful.... (p. 1)

Sometimes a literacy coach's work involves demonstrating faith for teachers. Fortunately, however, we have teachers to model our own trade. If we watch the amazing teachers in our building, we will learn how to believe, and we will find ourselves in a reciprocal sharing of faith.

Pursuing Joy

If we are not finding deep joy in our work, then we probably need to make a change: a change in practice, a change in philosophy, or a change in position. In *The Power of Full Engagement: Managing Energy, Not Time, Is the Key to High Performance and Personal Renewal*, Loehr and Schwartz (2003) write, "One of the most revealing questions that we ask the clients who come through our training is how frequently in their lives they experience a sense of joy or deep satisfaction" (p. 76). This is a valuable question and one that is difficult to answer.

I would suggest that we need to locate sources of joy in our work and cultivate them. We should support teachers as they investigate how it feels to be deeply joyful as well. Loehr and Schwartz go on to say that joy is born of "full engagement" which presents itself as "feeling eager to get to work in the morning, equally happy to return home in the evening and capable of setting clear boundaries between the two" (p. 5). How many of us, by this definition, can call ourselves joyful or fully engaged?

It is purely the nature of teaching to be overworked, and no one understands this unless they have lived it. I am not a violent person, but I would be embarrassed to write about what I'm inclined to do when someone says, "Oh, you're a teacher. That must be great. You get off at 3:30 and you don't have to work in the summer." The reality is that we cram a full-time, year-round, 8:00–5:00 job into 185 days. Then we spend much of our summers working in our schools and attending professional learning without pay. Mathematically and physically, of course, this doesn't work, and our bodies and our psyches pay the price.

Loehr and Schwartz (2003) began with athletes when they initiated their investigations into increasing joy and subsequent productivity. However, the fascinating thing about their work is that they didn't spend any time working on the technical or tactical skill of the athletes. They didn't work on their swings or their strokes or their pitches. They didn't help them run faster or jump higher. They write,

> Conventional wisdom holds that if you find talented people and equip them with the right skills for the challenge at hand, they will perform at their best. In our experience that often isn't so. Energy is the X factor that makes it possible to fully ignite talent and skill. (p. 7)

What if this is true for teachers? What if they don't need more strategies, more materials, and more procedures as much as they need more of the energy that is a byproduct of joy? What if having more joy and more energy would make most teachers better at their jobs? It is certainly worth exploring. This is not to say that teachers won't benefit from more strategies, more materials, and more procedures. I am simply saying that they can't fully take advantage of these things if a lack of joy has left them drained of energy.

This sense of deep joy from being fully engaged in the very present moment is something with which I have really struggled. I have always just been holding out for the next stimulus, looking forward to the event or to some kind of change. For a number of reasons I am now finding more joy in the present moment and avoiding reliance on that sense of anticipation that presents a false sense of contentment. Inevitably, once the anticipated event occurred, I had to find something else to anticipate.

My drive to do everything right has also challenged my sense of joy. Perfectionism is the enemy of joy because we always come up short when we are trying to be perfect. Joy should live independently of context, and it should manifest itself in an ability to look at a situation and know that it isn't the end of the world. I am better at this at some times than at others. Most days in this work I am joyful and optimistic. Children are truly reading better. Teachers are excited about the progress their students are making. I'm excited about the growing expertise of the teachers.

But some days all I can see is the torturously long road ahead of us. Student writing seems flat and student writers seem disfluent. I have miscommunicated with teachers and left them irritated. Some of our neediest students don't seem to be making progress. The district office has another time-consuming task for me. I feel overwhelmed by the volume and diversity of demands for my attention.

Literacy coaches have days when they want to go home and never come back and days when they don't want to leave the school. This emotional roller coaster is fatiguing. Even if we hold our hands up and scream with excitement on the way down the hill, we may find ourselves nauseous when it is all over. Most of the damage of our work manifests itself after the day's ride is over, and fatigue interferes with our personal time. The good news is that if we stay with it, if we teach ourselves to focus on the positive in ourselves and in teachers, if we identify and protect our margins and boundaries of time and energy, and if can view our shortcomings kindly, we can find joy in literacy coaching nine days out of 10. And on the tenth day the dismay will be less wearing because we know that tomorrow will probably be better.

There is tremendous potential for deep joy in our work. We have benefits that many professions don't. We get to work with children. Our work is intrinsically connected to a strong moral purpose. The field of education in general and the field of reading education specifically continue to develop a wider and stronger research base, and there are unlimited opportunities for learning and growth.

My hope is that you understand and experience deep joy in your personal and professional lives. You really don't know that you are missing joy until you see someone who has it. Joy is a relatively new acquaintance for me; I hope she is an old friend of yours. If not, she is someone worth knowing; consider yourself introduced now, and begin pursuing her.

Love in Unlikely Spaces

I will end this section on the love note. At the risk of sounding corny, I think that attachments with teachers can reach a level of affection akin to love. In *Walking on Water: Reading, Writing, and Revolution* (Jensen, 2004), I read about Jensen's work teaching writing to college students and prisoners: "The foundation of my work in the classroom remains the same for both college and prison, which is to respect and *love my students into* becoming who they are" (p. 33, emphasis added). I said to myself, "Well now, he just said what I have been thinking." We love them into it.

hooks (2000) describes love as something you do. Surely our actions announce our emotions. Think of love as something you do around your school, and nurture it as the soul of your work. This choice disentangles us from knots of emotion that attempt to dictate our behaviors. hooks writes, "To begin by always thinking of love as an action rather than a feeling is one way in which anyone using the word in this manner automatically assumes accountability and responsibility" (p. 13).

If we treat teachers like people we love, if our decision making and our communications all grow from this affection, then teachers will recognize our sincerity. This doesn't mean we don't encourage— sometimes even challenge—them to grow. It just means that we assume the best of them and honor them in our collaborations; we demonstrate respect, patience, care, and honesty.

I have come across little in my reading that has addressed the place of emotions in schools. Love, in particular, seems absent. However, if our work is too congested for love, we eliminate the possibilities for the long-term growth that is rooted in emotional spaces. Hargreaves and Fullan (1998) write, "Schools, where learning leaves little place for love, are schools without substance or soul" (p. 31).

In *The Power of Their Ideas: Lessons for America from a small school in Harlem*, Meier (1995) writes, "Caring and compassion are not soft, mushy goals. They are part of the hard core of subjects we are responsible for teaching" (p. 63). All of our work as coaches begins here. All of it. If we can't or won't care, we're in the wrong profession.

Calkins (1994) says, "convince your children that you love them, then there's nothing you can't teach them" (pp. 17–18). I believe this is true for all of us, including teachers. I found the idea of loving the teachers with whom I work very risky when I first began literacy coaching. I had just been through a number of difficult changes in my personal life. I was new to my town and new to the literacy coach role, and I wanted to keep my work on a professional level. I was fiercely determined not to get attached to the teachers in the building, nor did I intend to show them my personal side.

But this didn't work. If we invest our time and emotional energy in a group of people, we will grow to love them. If we find that we don't love them, then we probably haven't truly given of ourselves.

In the fall of my second year as a coach, a teacher with whom I had worked a lot told me that his doctor had found a lump on his prostate and on his colon. This was a young man, and I was struck by the news on two levels. First, I was devastated that he might be facing some serious health issues. I cried when he told me (probably not the response he needed from me). I cried when I saw him at a distance in the hall, and I cried when I went home and told my husband about what the doctors had found.

Second, I was surprised by how this news had affected me. Hadn't I decided not to let myself get attached? To keep everyone at a distance? To position myself only in an objective stance? This may have been my original intent. I learned, however, that even as I was consciously saying, "I'm going to keep my distance," with every interaction with teachers, even though they were all "professional," I was becoming more and more connected to them. Then their idiosyncrasies, their strengths, and their habits all became the makeup of people about whom I care immensely. We appreciate people for who they are. I think perhaps the teachers in my school came to think of my quirks and peculiarities in the same way, as part of a complete package that makes me who I am.

Many of us entered teaching because we love children; we have a passion for them. We want to make their lives richer, give them skills for living well, and help them appreciate the variety in our world. But these deep, passionate, and even emotional motivations that called many of us to the field of education are the very things we arm ourselves against now. Despite our efforts, the emotional aspects of our work are unavoidable. In fact, we are likely to be working in a building full of passionate, emotional, and dedicated people, and this can be complicated. Deep change requires an emotional investment. It is hard and honest and slow, and we cannot do it without spending ourselves and our emotional collateral.

Being of Service to Teachers

To work in a service profession is, by definition, to work toward our own extinction, and working to render ourselves unnecessary is the ultimate in moral purpose. The very act of doing our jobs should move us toward obsolescence, and this makes ours a purpose of service. I imagine that most literacy coaches would choose to have worldwide literacy today, even if it meant that tomorrow they would have to start from scratch professionally, and even at the risk of hardship to their own families. There is a sweet irony to all this. There is no higher moral purpose than that of sincere service.

In *The Heart of Coaching: Using Transformational Coaching to Create a High-Performance Culture* (Crane, 2002), Crane describes the type of service critical to coaching:

> Helpfulness has everything to do with intention. To be truly helpful means being able to set aside personal needs and to focus instead on the needs of others. The Transformational Coach learns that a service mindset is essential to coaching others. Helpfulness comes from the heart, not from the head. (p. 185)

To serve from the heart, we must let ourselves grow fond of the teachers with whom we work and let this fondness fuel our drive to be helpful.

So I don't feel as if I work for the school district. I don't feel as if I work for the state. I don't feel as though I work for my principal. While I answer to all three, my work is about service to teachers. "The leadership that counts, in the end, is the kind that touches people differently. It taps their emotions, appeals to their values, and responds to their connections with other people. It is morally based leadership—a form of stewardship" (Sergiovanni, 1992, p. 120). This is an easy thing to say, but to live it one must really believe it. Even then, it is easy for a literacy coach to veer off course. As I see it, there are two aspects of serving teachers that a literacy coach must keep in mind.

First, working in service to teachers requires protecting them. I must work to protect them from feeling overwhelmed by district policies, from becoming discouraged, from setting unfair expectations for themselves, and from taking care of their students before they take care of themselves. Many times teachers don't even know that you are advocating for them behind the scenes. However, care in the absence of empathy creates a paradox that simply portrays a literacy coach as unpredictable and untrustworthy. Neither of these traits will work in the favor of the teachers or children in the school.

For example, say that I am deliberate about asking teachers to do anything for me. If I am collecting materials or data, preparing for a literacy event, or preparing for professional learning, I try to take care of as much as I can on my own or with the help of volunteers. We are contradicting ourselves if we say we want to take care of teachers, and then we give them a list of things we need them to do.

Serving teachers by attempting to protect them from overload is not exactly a radical idea on paper. However, in terms of the realities of working, particularly in the field of education, it is heresy. Education is notorious for burning people out and it is rarely the children that push teachers over the edge, making them turn in their elementary school IDs and look for a temporary secretarial job. It is, rather, the committee meetings, the extra hours required to plan and prepare well, the paperwork, and the bureaucracy.

Sometimes I'm amazed that with school pictures, the spelling bee, the traveling dentist, Little League sign-up, Boy and Girl Scout recruitment, attendance, lunch counts, activities for parents, library overdue notices, lost library books, fire drills, tornado drills, lockdown drills, birthday parties, wrapping paper sales, candle sales, field trip money, wet pants, lost teeth, lost pencils, dull pencils, notes from parents, notes to parents, student agendas, homework, announcements, fevers, vomiting, and forgotten glasses teachers have any time at all to attend to the curriculum. Add to that public scrutiny, curriculum fluctuations, summative observations, lesson planning, textbook reviews, high-stakes testing, data analysis, professional learning, and faculty meetings and it becomes painfully clear that we need to take care of teachers because they are taking care of everyone and everything else. In the tidal wave of educational flotsam and jetsam, providing teachers with support, encouragement, and advocacy becomes our moral purpose, so that supporting, encouraging, and advocating for children can be theirs.

Making Room for Mystery in Our Lives

Educators, especially administrators, are usually concerned about instructional time, and certainly being good stewards of the time we have with teachers and children is worthwhile. I must admit I've invested a fair amount of my own energy in analyzing how classroom time is spent, all with the purpose of exorcising "wasted time" from the classroom. However, I have really begun to rethink this regimented definition of efficiency. I've begun to think that loose time, like spare change, can add up and contribute significantly to the recovery required to compensate for our constant expenditures of energy. Maybe putting some padding in our daily schedules will benefit the children as much as it does us.

In an article about children and time, Edwards (2005) writes about our cluttered schedules and the fact that there are planners and schedulers for children now. He suggests that much of the learning that affects us powerfully occurs outside the boundaries of the precisely scheduled lesson. He writes,

> A teacher may know what to cover in a lesson plan, but there's no way to plumb the mystery of what inspires curiosity.
>
> Relevance matters because teachers need to give their students real-world examples of the classroom's apparent abstractions. But irrelevance matters, too, because it offers food for unpredictable thought. After all, lives are formed at least as much by what is unplanned and accidental as by methodical plotting. (p. 9)

Once again, we are faced with trying to balance the seesaw between recovery in and out of the classroom and maintaining instructional time. If teachers are worried that someone is going to come in and check to see if they are on exactly the right page at exactly the right time of the day, if schools are overly committed to the idea of "bell-to-bell" teaching, and, if education treats educators as robots, then teachers and children are trying to accomplish more and more with less and less energy.

Souvenirs

The emotions we wear protect us from the weather of literacy coaching work. Stepping into the storm of educational change without outfitting ourselves in hope, faith, joy, and love promises to leave us nursing an emotional cold. On the other hand, if we make room for teachers and ourselves to feel at work, we tap into the potential for long-term learning that comes from uniting experience with emotion. The foundation that supports these emotional expressions is a literacy coach's service to teachers and an adherence to a moral purpose of supporting change without treading on teachers.

This book has been an effort to describe the work around a project that is still in progress, a tree that is still growing. This book, my most authentic experience with the writing process, has taught me that books don't stop growing either. It is a common understanding among writers that a document is never "finished"; one could spend an eternity laboring through revisions and always see more ways to make things better. I read somewhere once that children's author E.B. White ran after the mailman to make more changes to his just-mailed manuscript for *Charlotte's Web*.

An author's sense that a book can always be revised is not the only aspect of incompletion around writing. What I have learned is that, when you are writing a narrative about your life, the story continues moving forward despite the fact that you are trying to bring the book to a close. Because life continues moving forward, you have to stop a book rather than finish it.

When fluent readers read, their eyes are always a little bit ahead of their voices. This is referred to as eye–voice span. It seems that, with writing, there is a life–book span representing the time between when interesting things happen in life and the time you actually get them down on paper. Because I haven't finished literacy coaching and I am developing new ideas daily, it is hard to call this project finished. Every day I learn something new and often I think it is worth sharing. However, the contents of this book are a snapshot of our work at Chase Street, not a full-length film. So, while you are looking at this picture, we will be arranging new compositions, examining our evolving ideas through the lens of time, and thinking about our life some more.

Reproducible Forms

CLASSROOM VISITATION FEEDBACK FORM

Visitor							
Teacher		Date		Time In		Time Out	

Lesson	Guided Reading		Writer's Workshop		Working With Words	
	Shared Reading		Independent Reading		Read-Aloud	
	Other					

What the students were doing	What the teacher was doing
Students:	Texts:

Impact on Learning and Instructional Considerations: _____

_____

_____

_____

_____

_____

_____

LITERACY COACH EVALUATION

(1-strongly agree; 2-agree; 3-disagree; 4-strongly disagree)

1. When I have a problem, the literacy coach is helpful in developing a plan for addressing it.   1 2 3 4

2. When I ask for something, the literacy coach is prompt in responding to my requests.   1 2 3 4

3. I feel like the literacy coach listens to me.   1 2 3 4

4. I feel like the literacy coach respects my time.   1 2 3 4

5. I feel like I have grown in the area of reading instruction this year as a result of the staff development in which I have participated.   1 2 3 4

6. I feel like the literacy coach cares about me both as a person and as a teacher.   1 2 3 4

7. I feel like the literacy coach is interested in helping me grow as a teacher.   1 2 3 4

8. I feel like the literacy coach has a vision for this school.   1 2 3 4

9. I feel like the literacy coach communicates with us clearly.   1 2 3 4

10. The literacy coach is available when I need her.   1 2 3 4

I'm glad that my literacy coach _____

_____

_____

_____

I wish that my literacy coach would _____

_____

_____

_____

Some things we have addressed this year in the area of literacy with which I have been pleased are

_____

_____

_____

Some things we did not address this year in the area of literacy that we need to address next year are

_____

_____

_____

REFERENCES

Ada, A.F., & Campoy, F.I. (2004). *Authors in the classroom: A transformative education process*. Boston: Allyn & Bacon.

Allen, J. (2006). *Becoming a literacy leader: Supporting learning and change*. Portland, ME: Stenhouse.

Allen, J. (in press). *Diverse families, welcoming schools: Partnerships for learning*. New York: Teachers College Press.

Anderson, P.K. (2001). But what if...Supporting leaders and learners. *Phi Delta Kappan*, *82*, 737–740.

Applebaum, B. (2003). White privilege, complicity, and the social construction of race. *Educational Foundations*, *17*(4), 5–20.

Banks, J.A. (2001). Citizenship education and diversity: Implications for teacher education. *Journal of Teacher Education*, *52*, 5–16.

Barkley, S.G., with Bianco, T. (Contributing Ed.). (2005). *Quality teaching in a culture of coaching*. Lanham, MD: Scarecrow Education.

Barr, K., Simmons, B., & Zarrow, J. (2003, April). *School coaching in context: A case study in capacity building*. Paper presented at the annual meeting of the American Educational Research Association, Chicago, IL.

Betts, E.A. (1946). *Foundations of reading instruction: With emphasis on differentiated guidance*. New York: American Book Company.

Calkins, L.M. (1994). *The art of teaching writing* (New ed.). Portsmouth, NH: Heinemann.

Chubb, J.E., & Moe, T.M. (1990). *Politics, markets, and America's schools*. Washington, DC: Brookings Institution.

Clay, M.M. (1993). Reading Recovery: A guidebook for teachers in training. Portsmouth, NH: Heinemann.

Coskie, T., Robinson, L., Buly, M.R., & Egawa, K. (2005). What makes an effective literacy coach? *Voices From the Middle*, *12*(4), 60–61.

Covey, S.R. (1989). *The 7 habits of highly effective people: Powerful lessons in personal change*. New York: Simon & Schuster.

Crane, T.G. (2002). *The heart of coaching: Using transformational coaching to create a high-performance culture* (2nd ed.). San Diego, CA: FTA.

Delpit, L.D. (1992). Education in a multicultural society: Our future's greatest challenge. *The Journal of Negro Education*, *61*, 237–249.

Delpit, L.D. (1995). Teachers, culture, and power: An interview with Lisa Delpit. In D.P. Levine, R. Lowe, R. Peterson, & R. Tenorio (Eds.), *Rethinking schools: An agenda for change* (pp. 136–147). New York: New Press.

Dillard, A. (1989). *The writing life*. New York: HarperCollins.

DuFour, R. (2002). The learning-centered principal. *Educational Leadership, 59*(8), 12–15.

Edelsky, C. (2003). Theory, politics, hope and action. *National Writing Project Quarterly, 25*(3), 10–14.

Edwards, O. (2005, February/March). Editor's note. *Edutopia*, p. 9.

Ehrenreich, B. (2001). *Nickel and dimed: On (not) getting by in America*. New York. Metropolitan.

Elkonin, D.B. (1973). In J. Downing (Ed.), *Comparative reading: Cross-national studies of behavior and processes in reading and writing* (pp. 551–559). New York: Macmillan.

Elmore, R.F. (2002). *Bridging the gap between standards and achievement: The imperative for professional development in education*. Washington, DC: Albert Shanker Institute.

Even-Ascencio, J. (2002). *Coaching to support ongoing school-wide professional learning: Promises and problems of on-site professional development*. Unpublished master's thesis, Harvard University, Cambridge, MA.

Freire, P. (1994). *Pedagogy of hope: Reliving Pedagogy of the Oppressed* (R.R. Barr, Trans.). New York: Continuum.

Frey, N., & Kelly, P.R. (2002). The effects of staff development, modeling, and coaching of interactive writing on instructional repertoires of K–1 teachers in a professional development school. In D.L. Schallert, C.M. Fairbanks, J. Worthy, B. Maloch, & J.V. Hoffman (Eds.), *51st yearbook of the National Reading Conference* (pp. 176–185). Oak Creek, WI: National Reading Conference.

Fullan, M. (2001). *Leading in a culture of change*. San Francisco: Jossey-Bass.

Galm, R., & Perry, G.S., Jr. (2004). Coaching moves beyond the gym: Successful site-based coaching offers lessons. *Journal of Staff Development, 25*, 1–4.

Garmston, R., Linder, C., & Whitaker, J. (2003). Reflections on cognitive coaching. *Educational Leadership, 51*(2), 57–61.

Gay, G. (2000). *Culturally responsive teaching: Theory, research, & practice*. New York: Teachers College Press.

Gladwell, M. (2005). *Blink: The power of thinking without thinking*. Boston: Little, Brown.

Goleman, D. (1995). *Emotional intelligence: Why it can matter more than IQ*. New York: Bantam.

González, N., Moll, L.C., & Amanti, C. (Eds.). (2005). *Funds of knowledge: Theorizing practices in households, communities, and classrooms*. Mahwah, NJ: Erlbaum.

Guiney, E. (2001). Coaching isn't just for athletes: The role of teacher leaders. *Phi Delta Kappan, 82*, 740–743.

Hall, B. (2004). Literacy coaches: An evolving role. *Carnegie Reporter, 3*(1). Retrieved September 8, 2006, from http://www.carnegie.org/reporter/09/literacy/index.html

Hargreaves, A., & Fullan, M. (1998). *What's worth fighting for out there?* New York: Teachers College Press.

Hargreaves, A., & Fullan, M. (2000). Mentoring in the new millennium. *Theory Into Practice, 39*, 50–56.

Heifetz, R.A., & Laurie, D.L. (1997). The work of leadership. *Harvard Business Review, 75*, 124–134.

Hogan, R., Raskin, R., & Fazzini, D. (1990). The dark side of charisma. In K.E.Clark & M.B. Clark (Eds.), *Measures of leadership* (pp. 343–354). West Orange, NJ: Leadership Library of America.

hooks, b. (1994). *Outlaw culture: Resisting representations*. New York: Routledge.

hooks, b. (1995). *Killing rage: Ending racism*. New York: Henry Holt.

hooks, b. (2000). *All about love: New visions*. New York: William Morrow.

hooks, b. (2001). *Salvation: Black people and love*. New York: William Morrow.

hooks, b. (2003). *Teaching community: A pedagogy of hope*. New York: Routledge.

Hopkins, D. (1990). Integrating staff development and school improvement: A study of teacher personality and school climate. In B.R. Joyce (Ed.), *Changing school culture through staff development* (pp. 41–67). Alexandria, VA: Association for Supervision and Curriculum Development.

Ingersoll, R.M., & Smith, T.M. (2003). The wrong solution to the teacher shortage. *Educational Leadership, 60*(8), 30–33.

International Reading Association (IRA). (2004). *The role and qualifications of the reading coach in the United States* (Position statement). Newark, DE: Author. Retrieved November 30, 2006, from http://www.reading.org/downloads/positions/ps1065_reading_coach.pdf

International Reading Association (IRA). (2006). *Standards for middle and high school literacy coaches* . Newark, DE: Author. Retrieved November 30, 2006, from http://www.reading.org/downloads/resources/597coaching_standards.pdf

International Reading Association (IRA), Professional Standards and Ethics Committee. (2004). *Standards for reading professionals—Revised 2003*. Newark, DE: Author. Retrieved November 30, 2006, from http://www.reading.org/resources/issues/reports/professional_standards.html

IRA surveys coaches. (2006, April/May). *Reading Today, 23*, 1–3.

Irvine, J.J. (2003). *Educating teachers for diversity: Seeing with a cultural eye*. New York: Teachers College Press.

Iyer, A., Leach, C.W., & Pedersen, A. (2004). Racial wrongs and restitutions: The role of guilt and other group-based emotions. In M. Fine, L. Weis, L.P. Pruitt, & A. Burns (Eds.), *Off white: Readings on power, privilege, and resistance* (2nd ed., pp. 345–361). New York: Routledge.

Jensen, D. (2004). *Walking on water: Reading, writing, and revolution*. White River Junction, VT: Chelsea Green.

Johnston, P.H. (2004). *Choice words: How our language affects children's learning*. Portland, ME: Stenhouse.

Joyce, B.R. (2004). How are professional learning communities created? History has a few messages. *Phi Delta Kappan, 86*, 76–83.

Joyce, B.R., Murphy, C., Showers, B., & Murphy, J. (1989). School renewal as cultural change. *Educational Leadership, 47*(3), 70–77.

Joyce, B.R., & Showers, B. (1980). Improving inservice training: The messages of research. *Educational Leadership, 37*(5), 379–385.

Joyce, B.R., & Showers, B. (1982). The coaching of teaching. *Educational Leadership, 40*(1), 4–8, 10.

Joyce, B.R., & Showers, B. (2002). *Student achievement through staff development.* Alexandria, VA: Association for Supervision and Curriculum Development.

Joyce, B.R., Showers, B., & Rolheiser-Bennett, C. (1987). Staff development and student learning: A synthesis of research on models of teaching. *Educational Leadership, 45*(2), 11–23.

Killion, J. (2003). Use these 6 keys to open doors to literacy: Study of what works by NSDC and NEA distills principles for success support. *Journal of Staff Development, 24*(2), 10–16.

Knight, J. (2004). Instructional coaches make progress through partnership: Intensive support can improve teaching. *Journal of Staff Development, 25*(2), 32–37.

Knight, J. (2005). A primer on instructional coaches. *Principal Leadership, 5*(9), 16–21.

Kohler, F.W., Crilley, K.M., Shearer, D.D., & Good, G. (1997). Effects of peer coaching on teacher and student outcomes. *Journal of Educational Research, 90,* 240–250.

Kübler-Ross, E. (1969). *On death and dying: What the dying have to teach doctors, nurses, clergy, and their own families.* New York: Macmillan.

Lashway, L. (1998). Creating a learning organization. *ERIC Digest, 121,* 1–2.

Lawrence, S.M., & Tatum, B.D. (2004). White educators as allies: Moving from awareness to action. In M. Fine, L. Weis, L.P. Pruitt, & A. Burns (Eds.), *Off white: Readings on power, privilege, and resistance* (2nd ed., pp. 362–372). New York: Routledge.

Learning Point Associates. (2004). *Reading First coaching: A guide for coaches and Reading First leaders* (White paper). Naperville, IN: Author. Retrieved November 30, 2006, from http://www.learningpt.org/pdfs/literacy/coachesguide.pdf

Leonard, L., & Leonard, P. (2003). The continuing trouble with collaboration: Teachers talk. *Current Issues in Education, 6*(15). Retrieved September 29, 2006, from http://cie.ed.asu.edu/volume6/number15

Loehr, J.E., & Schwartz, T. (2003). *The power of full engagement: Managing energy, not time, is the key to high performance and personal renewal.* New York: Free Press.

Lyons, C.A., & Pinnell, G.S. (2001). *Systems for change in literacy education: A guide to professional development.* Portsmouth, NH: Heinemann.

Marks, S.U., & Gersten, R. (1998). Engagement and disengagement between special and general educators: An application of Miles and Huberman's cross-case analysis. *Learning Disability Quarterly, 21*(1), 34–56.

Marx, S., & Pennington, J. (2003). Pedagogies of critical race theory: Experimentations with white preservice teachers. *International Journal of Qualitative Studies in Education, 16*(1), 91–110.

Mayo Clinic. (2006). *Stress: Unhealthy response to the pressures of life.* Retrieved October 2, 2006, from http://www.mayoclinic.com/health/stress/SR00001

McAllister, E.A., & Neubert, G.A. (1995). *New teachers helping new teachers: Preservice peer coaching*. Bloomington, IN: ERIC/EDInfo Press.

McAndrew, D.A. (2005). *Literacy leadership. Six strategies for peoplework*. Newark, DE: International Reading Association.

McIntosh, P. (1990). White privilege: Unpacking the invisible knapsack. *Independent School, 49*(2), 31–36.

Meier, D. (1995). *The power of their ideas: Lessons for America from a small school in Harlem*. Boston: Beacon Press.

Michalove, B. (1999). Circling in: Examining prejudice in history and in ourselves. In J. Allen (Ed.), *Class actions: Teaching for social justice in elementary and middle school* (pp. 21–33). New York: Teachers College Press.

Miner, B. (1995). Taking multicultural, anti-racist education seriously: An interview with Enid Lee. In D. Levine, R. Lowe, B. Peterson, & R. Tenorio (Eds.), *Rethinking schools: An agenda for change* (pp. 9–16). New York: The New Press.

Moll, L.C., Amanti, C., Neff, D., & González, N. (1992). Funds of knowledge for teaching: Using a qualitative approach to connect homes and classrooms. *Theory Into Practice, 31*, 132–141.

Moody, K. (1997). *Workers in a lean world: Unions in the international economy*. New York: Verso.

Morgenstern, J. (2004). *Making work* work: *New strategies for surviving and thriving at the office*. New York: Simon & Schuster.

National Institutes of Health. (2002). *Stress system malfunction could lead to serious, life threatening disease*. Retrieved October 2, 2006, from http://www.nih.gov/news/pr/sep 2002/nichd-09.htm

Nieto, S. (1999). *The light in their eyes: Creating multicultural learning communities*. New York: Teachers College Press.

No Child Left Behind Act of 2001, Pub. L. No. 107-110, 115 Stat. 1425 (2002).

Pearson, P.D., & Gallagher, M.C. (1983). The instruction of reading comprehension. *Contemporary Educational Psychology, 8*(3), 317–344.

Perkins, S.J. (1998). On becoming a peer coach: Practices, identities, and beliefs of inexperienced coaches. *Journal of Curriculum and Supervision, 13*(3), 235–254.

Pinnell, G.S., & Lyons, C. (1998). *Literacy coordinator as instructional leader: The development of technical knowledge and skill*. Unpublished manuscript, The Ohio State University, Columbus, OH.

Quinn, B. (2001). *Snap, crackle, or stop: Change your career and shape your own destiny*. Cambridge, MA: Perseus.

Ray, K.W. (1999). *Wondrous words: Writers and writing in the elementary classroom*. Urbana, IL: National Council of Teachers of English.

Reeves, R. (2001). *Happy Mondays: Putting the pleasure back into work*. Cambridge, MA: Perseus.

Ritchie, J.S. (2006, January). *Crucial introspection: Interrogating whiteness in preservice teachers*. Paper presented at the Qualitative Interest Group, Athens, GA.

Robb, L. (2000). *Redefining staff development: A collaborative model for teachers and administrators.* Portsmouth, NH. Heinemann.

Sapolsky, R.M. (1994). *Why zebras don't get ulcers: A guide to stress, stress related diseases, and coping.* New York: W.H. Freeman.

Scarr, S. (1992). Developmental theories for the 1990s: Development and individual differences. *Child Development, 63,* 1–19.

Schmoker, M. (2004). At odds: Strategic planning—Learning communities at the crossroads: Toward the best schools we've ever had. *Phi Delta Kappan, 86*(1), 84–88.

Scott, S. (2002). *Fierce conversations: Achieving success at work and in life, one conversation at a time.* New York: Viking Press.

Sergiovanni, T.J. (1992). *Moral leadership: Getting to the heart of school improvement.* San Francisco: Jossey-Bass.

Showers, B. (1984). *Peer coaching: A strategy for facilitating transfer of training.* Eugene, OR: Center for Educational Policy and Management.

Showers, B. (1985). Teachers coaching teachers. *Educational Leadership, 42*(7), 43–48.

Showers, B., & Joyce, B. (1996). The evolution of peer coaching. *Educational Leadership, 53*(6), 12–16.

Showers, B., Joyce, B., & Bennett, B. (1987). Synthesis of research on staff development: A framework for future study and a stage-of-the-art analysis. *Educational Leadership, 45*(3), 77–87.

Slater, C.L., & Simmons, D.L. (2001). The design and implementation of a peer coaching program. *American Secondary Education, 29*(3), 67–76.

Snyder, T.D., Tan, A.G., & Hoffman, C.M. (2006). *Digest of education statistics, 2005* (NCES 2006-030). Washington, DC: U.S. Department of Education, National Center for Education Statistics.

Strizek, G.A., Pittsonberger, J.L., Riordan, K.E., Lyter, D.M., & Orlofsky, G.F. (2006). *Characteristics of schools, districts, teachers, principals, and school libraries in the United States: 2003–04 Schools and staffing survey* (NCES 2006-313 Revised). Washington, DC: U.S. Department of Education, National Center for Education Statistics.

Symonds, K.W. (2003). Three ways to fund literacy coaching. *Journal of Staff Development, 24*(4), 54–58.

Tatum, B.D. (1997). *"Why are all the Black kids sitting together in the cafeteria?" and other conversations about race.* New York: Basic Books.

Titone, C. (1998). Educating the White teacher as ally. In J.L. Kincheloe, S.R. Steinberg, N.M. Rodriguez, & R.E. Chennault (Eds.), *White reign: Deploying Whiteness in America* (pp. 159–175). New York: St. Martin's.

Toll, C.A. (2004). Separating coaching from supervising. *English Leadership Quarterly, 27*(2), 5–7.

Toll, C.A. (2005). *The literacy coach's survival guide: Essential questions and practical answers.* Newark, DE: International Reading Association.

Valdés, G. (1996). *Con respeto: Bridging the distances between culturally diverse families and schools: An ethnographic portrait.* New York: Teachers College Press.

Wenger, E.C., & Snyder, W.M. (2000). Communities of practice: The organizational frontier. *Harvard Business Review, 78*(1), 139–145.

Wheatley, M.J. (2002). *Turning to one another: Simple conversations to restore hope to the future*. San Francisco: Berrett-Koehler.

Literary References

Adams, H. (1999). *The education of Henry Adams*. New York: Oxford University Press.

Angelou, M. (1983). *I know why the caged bird sings*. New York: Bantam.

Baylor, B. (1986). *I'm in charge of celebrations*. Ill. P. Parnall. New York: Simon & Schuster.

Dobyns, S. (1996). The Ionius monk. In S. Dobyns, *Common carnage* (pp. 77–78). New York: Penguin.

Fox, M.J. (2002). *Lucky man: A memoir*. New York: Hyperion.

Nearing, H. (1992). "Twilight and evening star." In H. Nearing, *Loving and leaving the good life* (pp. 166–194). Post Mills, VT: Chelsea Green.

Strand, M. (1990). "The way it is." In *Selected poems by Mark Strand* (p. 81). New York: Alfred A. Knopf.

Twain, M. (2000). "The art of composition." In Neider, C. (Ed.), *Life as I find it: A treasury of Mark Twain rarities* (pp. 227–228). Lanham, MD: Cooper Square.

Vidal, G. (1993). *United States: Essays 1952–1992*. New York: Broadway Books.

INDEX

Note. Page numbers followed by *f* or *t* indicate figures or tables, respectively.

EMOTION(S): balancing with professionalism, 14, 193–194; of coaching, 182–197; of memory and learning, 183–194; skill with, coach and, 34–35, 66
ENGAGEMENT: and joy, 190–191
ENVIRONMENT: children and, 25–26; creating, 25–47, 55–56
ERROR: learning from, 53–54
EVALUATION: of literacy coaches, 151–155, 203. *See also* assessment
EVEN-ASCENCIO, J., 26
EXPERTISE: administrators and, 39; coach and, 16, 34

F

FAITH, 188–190
FAZZINI, D., 66
FEEDBACK, 125–133; examples of, 134t; forms, 125–126, 127f–128f, 202–203; on literacy coaching, 151–155; word choice for, 126–133
FLEXIBILITY: importance of, 20–21
FOX, M.J., 181
FREIRE, P., 186
FREY, N., 105
FULLAN, M., ix–x, 54, 70, 183–184, 186, 188, 190, 193

G

GALLAGHER, M.C., 107
GALM, R., 27
GARMSTON, R., 137
GAY, G., 175
GERSTEN, R., 89
GLADWELL, M., 176
GOLEMAN, D., 66
GONZÁLEZ, N., 177
GOOD: term, 130
GOOD, G., 187
GOODWILL: assumption of, 77–79
GOSSIP: limiting, 72–73
GRIEF: stages of, 171–177
GROWTH: pushing for, 12
GUILT: over racism, 172–173
GUINEY, E., 33, 129
GWYTHER, PEG, 77, 120

H

HABITS: positive, practicing, 58–59
HALL, B., 29
HALL, DAPHNE, 115–116
HARD WORK: versus perfectionism, 53
HARGREAVES, A., 183–184, 186, 188, 190, 193
HEIFETZ, R.A., 150
HILL, P., ix
HOFFMAN, C.M., 160
HOGAN, R., 66
HOME LIFE: balance with work life, 14; as self-care, 58; transitions to/from, 60–61
HONESTY: versus perfectionism, 52–53
HOOKS, B., 161, 165, 168, 173–174, 187, 193
HOPE, 186–188
HOPKINS, D., 67
HUMILITY: and feedback, 129

I

IMPROVEMENT: versus perfectionism, 52
INDEPENDENCE: teaching toward, 101–118
INDIVIDUALITY: versus consistency, 12; versus district initiatives, 13; space for, 113–114
INGERSOLL, R.M., 49
INITIATING PHASE: of learning, 107–110, 108t, 109f
INSTRUCTION: and administrator relationships, 39–40; coaches and, 31; data and, 145–149;
    effective, elements requiring coaching, 33–36, 35f, 105, 106f; skill at, coach and, 107
INTEGRITY: coach and, 34–35
INTERNATIONAL READING ASSOCIATION, 28–29, 34; Professional Standards and Ethics Committee,
    29
INVENTING PHASE: of learning, 108t, 109f, 111–112
INVITATION TO CLASSROOM: self-issued, 138–139; from teacher, 137–138
IRA SURVEYS COACHES, 30, 34
IRVINE, J.J., 160
ISOLATION, 187
IYER, A., 172

J

JENSEN, D., 68, 192
JOHNSTON, P.H., 52, 130, 132, 184
JOY, 17, 190–192
JOYCE, B.R., 26, 28, 34, 36, 77, 85, 112, 124, 128–129
JUDGMENT: in feedback, 131–132

K

KELLY, P.R., 105
KILLION, J., 103
KNIGHT, J., 29, 87, 114
KNOWLEDGE: versus expertise, 34; funds of, 177
KOHLER, F.W., 187
KÜBLER-ROSS, E., 171

L

LANGUAGE: of classroom visitation, 119–139; monitoring, 19
LASHWAY, L., 148
LAURIE, D.L., 150
LAWRENCE, S.M., 176
LEACH, C.W., 172
LEADERSHIP: coach versus teacher and, 11; and emotions, 66, 183; service as, 195; without
    authority, 40–45
LEADING EDGE, 132
LEARNING: emotions of, 183–194; phases of, 107–112, 108t, 109f; priorities for, 104–107;
    support for, 101–118
LEARNING COMMUNITY: emotions and, 187
LEARNING POINT ASSOCIATES, 124
LEONARD, L., 187
LEONARD, P., 187
LIKE: term, 131
LIMITATIONS: recognizing, as self-care, 59
LINDER, C., 137
LISTENING, 69–70; levels of, 70
LITERACY: visions of, 84–86

TOLL, C.A., 40, 59, 92–93
TRUTH: problems with, 79–80
TWAIN, M., 119

U
UNDERSTANDING: coaching toward, 10

V
VALDÉS, G., 167
VIDAL, G., 140
VISION: of literacy, 84–86; in school community, 86–87
VISITATION. *See* classroom visitation

W
WENGER, E.C., 54
WHEATLEY, M.J., 59, 89
WHITAKER, J., 137
WHITE, E.B., 199
WHITES: definition of, 162; privileges of, 165–166, 169–170; racial-identity development of, 163–169
WILLIAMSON, HALLIE, 51
WORD CHOICES: evaluation of, 133, 134*t*; for feedback, 126–133; for interactions, 132–133; monitoring, 19
WORK LIFE: balance with home life, 14; margins in, 56; transitions to/from, 60–61

Z
ZARROW, J., 67